LAW, CRIME AND LAW ENFORCEMENT

POLICE USE OF FORCE AND FEDERAL TACTICAL TEAMS

BACKGROUND AND CONSIDERATIONS

LAW, CRIME AND LAW ENFORCEMENT

Additional books in this series can be found on Nova's website
under the Series tab.

Additional e-books in this series can be found on Nova's website
under the e-book tab.

LAW, CRIME AND LAW ENFORCEMENT

POLICE USE OF FORCE AND FEDERAL TACTICAL TEAMS

BACKGROUND AND CONSIDERATIONS

BEVERLY GUZMAN
EDITOR

nova publishers
New York

Library of Congress Cataloging-in-Publication Data

ISBN: 978-1-63484-557-1

Published by Nova Science Publishers, Inc. † New York

CONTENTS

PREFACE

Several high-profile police shootings and other law enforcement-related deaths in the United States have sparked intense protests throughout the country and a fierce debate in Congress concerning the appropriate level of force police officers should wield in a society that equally values public safety and the lives of each of its citizens under law. These incidents have been the subject of several congressional hearings, have prompted the introduction of various legislative measures, and have catalyzed a new civil rights movement in the United States aimed at reforming the criminal justice system. Reformers claim that police work too closely with local prosecutors resulting in insufficient oversight and have called for greater involvement by the federal government. The law enforcement community and its supporters have countered that these recent deaths are anomalous in otherwise exemplary police conduct, and that placing the federal government in direct regulation of state and local police would present an unwarranted intrusion into state and local affairs. To provide legal context for this debate, this book will address three overarching questions: what are the constitutional rules governing an officer's use of force; what role has Congress played in providing a remedy for a violation of these rules; and what are the potential reforms to these rules and remedies? The authors of this book advocate for democratic ideals within law enforcement to combat the mindset that law enforcement officers are at war with the people they serve.

In: Police Use of Force …
Editor: Beverly Guzman

ISBN: 978-1-63484-557-1

Chapter 1

POLICE USE OF FORCE: RULES, REMEDIES AND REFORMS*

Richard M. Thompson

SUMMARY

Several high-profile police shootings and other law enforcement-related deaths in the United States have sparked intense protests throughout the country and a fierce debate in Congress concerning the appropriate level of force police officers should wield in a society that equally values public safety and the lives of each of its citizens under law. These incidents have been the subject of several congressional hearings, have prompted the introduction of various legislative measures, and have catalyzed a new civil rights movement in the United States aimed at reforming the criminal justice system. Reformers claim that police work too closely with local prosecutors resulting in insufficient oversight and have called for greater involvement by the federal government. The law enforcement community and its supporters have countered that these recent deaths are anomalous in otherwise exemplary police conduct, and that placing the federal government in direct regulation of state and local police would present an unwarranted intrusion into state and local affairs.

To provide legal context for this debate, this report will address three overarching questions: (1) what are the constitutional rules governing an

---

* This is an edited, reformatted and augmented version of a Congressional Research Service publication R44256, prepared for Members and Committees of Congress, dated October 30, 2015.

officer's use of force; (2) what role has Congress played in providing a remedy for a violation of these rules; and (3) what are the potential reforms to these rules and remedies?

Rules. In a line of cases beginning in the mid-1980s, the Supreme Court ruled that all claims of excessive force occurring during an arrest or investigatory stop—deadly or otherwise—are governed by the Fourth Amendment's prohibition against unreasonable seizures. Under prevailing judicial precedent, all uses of force must be "objectively reasonable" based on the totality of the circumstances viewed through the lens of the officer in the field. This requires a fact-intensive inquiry that is not easily reduced to categorical rules, but some general trends can be discerned from the case law. For instance, the courts have been deferential to officers in the field who are required to make split-second decisions in dangerous situations. Also, officers need not use the least intrusive means to effectuate a seizure so long as their actions are reasonable.

Remedies. In an effort to provide teeth to federal constitutional restraints, Congress has enacted three federal statutes that accord various remedies for police use of excessive force. First is the federal criminal statute, 18 U.S.C. § 242, which prohibits officers from willfully depriving another of a constitutional right while acting under color of law. Enacted shortly after the Civil War, many have argued that Section 242's specific intent *mens rea* requirement is too high a threshold to provide an adequate deterrence to excessive force. Moreover, the federal circuit courts are split on how to apply this test, with some requiring a strict form of intent and others permitting a reckless disregard jury instruction. Second is the federal civil rights statute, 42 U.S.C. § 1983, which provides a civil cause of action for deprivations of one's constitutional rights. While generally viewed as successful in providing monetary damages to those injured by officers in the field, the doctrine of qualified immunity has frequently shielded officers from liability when the law was not "clearly established" at the time. Third is the more recently enacted "pattern or practice" statute, 42 U.S.C. § 14141, which authorizes the Attorney General to sue local municipalities whose police forces have engaged in a pattern of excessive force under the Fourth Amendment.

Reforms. Various reform bills have been introduced in the 114th Congress to provide additional restraints on police use of force, including the Excessive Use of Force Prevention Act of 2015 (H.R. 2052), which would criminalize the use of chokeholds, and the Police Accountability Act of 2015 (H.R. 1102), which would create a new federal crime for certain homicides committed by law enforcement officers. Additionally, several bills would place requirements on states to report use of force statistics to the federal government.

INTRODUCTION

By the very nature of their job, law enforcement officers are tasked with using physical force to restrain individuals and protect themselves and others from harm.[1] Police officers must stop and seize violent suspects, serve search warrants in hostile environments, and maintain the peace and safety of the communities in which they serve. As then-Justice Rehnquist observed, "[p]olicemen on the beat are exposed, in the service of society, to all the risks which the constant effort to prevent crime and apprehend criminals entails: Because these people are literally the foot soldiers of society's defense of ordered liberty, the State has an especial interest in their protection."[2] However, a number of recent high-profile police shootings and other law enforcement-related deaths have reignited the debate about how much force police should wield in a democratic society that values both law and order and the personal liberty of each of its citizens under law.[3]

The shooting of Michael Brown by a Ferguson, Missouri police officer in the summer 2014 served as a flashpoint for this debate,[4] but it is just one in a spate of recent law enforcement-related deaths.[5] These deaths, and others, have prompted a call for legal accountability against the officers involved in these killings, but also, more broadly, for systemic police reform on both the federal and state level. President Obama responded by establishing the *Task Force on 21st Century Policing* in December 2014 to develop best policing practices and recommendations.[6] The task force's final report issued in May 2015 offered a set of policy recommendations focused on training, investigations, prosecutions, data collection, and information sharing. Similarly, the House Judiciary Committee held a hearing on policing strategies on May 19, 2015,[7] and various measures have been introduced in the 114th Congress to address both use of force tactics and data collection by state and local police departments. The public, too, has been thoroughly engaged on this issue. "Black Lives Matter," a movement that sprung up in response to the Treyvon Martin shooting and other police-related deaths, has recently released an initiative called "Campaign Zero," which contains a set of policy proposals to limit police use of excessive force, including a call for a national standard governing the use of deadly force and better reporting requirements on instances of excessive force by law enforcement officers.[8]

These reforms prompt the perennial debate concerning the role of Congress in addressing police reform, especially on the local level, where many of these deaths have occurred. Certain segments of the law enforcement community and its supporters have argued that regulating local police is best left to the province of state and local governments, and that a one-size-fits-all approach would hamper local experimentation.[9] Proponents of reform have countered that federal intervention is warranted as state and local governments and police departments have not adequately held their officers legally accountable for the improper use of force.

Insofar as *constitutional* violations are concerned, there is historical precedent for congressional intervention. Shortly after the Civil War, Congress enacted two federal statutes—one criminal and one civil—to provide legal remedies for newly freed African Americans who were being deprived of their civil rights. On the civil side is 42 U.S.C. § 1983, which provides individuals with a civil cause of action to recover damages for the deprivation of such rights.[10] On the criminal side is 18 U.S.C. § 242, which makes it a federal crime to willfully deprive someone of his constitutional rights.[11] Of more recent vintage (1994) is 42 U.S.C. § 14141, which permits the Department of Justice (DOJ) to sue local police departments that engage in a "pattern or practice" of constitutional violations, including the use of excessive force.[12]

To provide legal context for this debate, this report will address three overarching questions: (1) what are the constitutional rules governing an officer's use of force; (2) what role has Congress played in providing a remedy for a violation of these rules; and (3) what are the potential reforms to these rules and remedies?

RULES GOVERNING USE OF FORCE

The first question that must be addressed is what rules govern police use of force.[13] Because the majority of recent law enforcement-related deaths have arisen in the context of street encounters with police (rather than pre- or post-trial detention), this report will focus almost exclusively on the Fourth Amendment right to be free from unreasonable seizures, which governs such encounters.[14]

Fourth Amendment "Objective Reasonableness"

The Fourth Amendment guarantees "the right of the people to be secure in their persons, houses, papers, and effects, from unreasonable searches and seizures."[15] While this provision is best known for providing restraints on government searches and surveillance and the procedures under which they may be conducted, in a series of cases beginning in the 1980s the Supreme Court interpreted the Fourth Amendment as the primary federal legal restraint on excessive force. Prior to these cases, the lower circuit and district courts largely applied the substantive component of the Due Process Clause to all claims of excessive force, deadly or otherwise.[16] However, in *Tennessee v. Garner* and *Graham v. Connor*, the Court grounded all excessive force claims in the Fourth Amendment's right to be free from unreasonable seizures.[17]

Deadly Force under Tennessee v. Garner

In the 1985 case *Tennessee v. Garner*, the Court assessed whether Tennessee's deadly force statute—which, like those of other states at the time, permitted police to use deadly force to shoot a fleeing felon—passed constitutional muster.[18] In that case, police were responding to a reported burglary when an officer at the scene saw a young African American male fleeing the back of the house, apparently unarmed.[19] In an effort to prevent his escape, the officer yelled for the suspect to halt and, when he failed to do so, shot him in the back of the head as he was climbing over a fence. The shot was fatal.

The victim's family brought a civil suit under Section 1983 for the alleged violation of the deceased's constitutional rights. The federal district and circuit courts both held that the officer had acted in good faith on Tennessee's use of force statute, which provided that "[i]f, after notice of the intention to arrest the defendant, he either flee or forcibly resist, the officer may use all the necessary means to effect the arrest."[20] In a 6-3 decision authored by Justice White, the Supreme Court reversed and held that the use of deadly force against a fleeing felon is unconstitutional.

Fourth Amendment protections.[21] To determine a seizure's reasonableness, a reviewing court must "balance the nature and quality of the intrusion on the individual's Fourth Amendment interests against the importance of the governmental interests alleged to justify the intrusion."[22] On the individual's side of the ledger, the Court noted that the "intrusiveness of a seizure by means of deadly force is unmatched."[23] On the government's side, the Court highlighted the government's various law enforcement interests, including arresting suspects peacefully without putting the public at risk. Balancing these interests, the Court ultimately held that the "use of deadly force to prevent the escape of all felony suspects, whatever the circumstances, is constitutionally unreasonable."[24] Rather than furthering the goals of the criminal justice process, Justice White noted that killing a suspect ensures that this system will never be put in motion as the government cannot bring a deceased person to justice. While rejecting the application of deadly force against an individual for merely committing a felony, the opinion went on to describe when such force is permissible:

> Where the officer has probable cause to believe that the suspect poses a threat of serious physical harm, either to the officer or to others, it is not constitutionally unreasonable to prevent escape by using deadly force. Thus, if the suspect threatens the officer with a weapon or there is probable cause to believe that he has committed a crime involving the infliction or threatened infliction of serious physical harm, deadly force may be used if necessary to prevent escape, and if, where feasible, some warning has been given.[25]

Note that *Garner* arose in the context of the use of *deadly* force. Four years later, the Court in *Graham v. Connor* addressed whether this same rule should extend to the use of *non*-deadly force.[26]

All Uses of Force under Graham v. Connor

In *Graham v. Connor*, police officers pulled over an individual suspected of shoplifting.[27] In response to his erratic behavior, one of the officers forcefully slammed him on the hood of a police cruiser and threw him headfirst into the car. The suspect sustained significant injuries and sued the police for excessive force under Section 1983.

Resolving a dispute in the lower federal courts about whether the Fourth Amendment applied outside the context of deadly force, the Supreme Court held that "*all* claims that law enforcement officers have used excessive force—deadly or not—in the course of an arrest, investigatory stop, or other 'seizure' of a free citizen should be analyzed under the Fourth Amendment and its 'reasonableness' standard."[28] Writing for the Court, Chief Justice Rehnquist observed that "[t]he test of reasonableness under the Fourth Amendment is not capable of precise definition or mechanical application."[29] Instead, "its proper application requires careful attention to the facts and circumstances of each particular case, including the severity of the crime at issue, whether the suspect poses an immediate threat to the safety of the officers or others, and whether he is actively resisting arrest or attempting to evade arrest by flight."[30] These three factors have taken on considerable importance in use of force jurisprudence in the lower courts.

Additionally, Chief Justice Rehnquist described the interpretive lens through which excessive force cases must be viewed. First, the "'reasonableness' of a particular use of force must be judged from the perspective of a reasonable officer on the scene, rather than with the 20/20 vision of hindsight."[31] Second, the "calculus of reasonableness must embody allowance for the fact that police officers are often forced to make split-second judgments—in circumstances that are tense, uncertain, and rapidly evolving—about the amount of force that is necessary in a particular situation."[32] Finally, the reasonableness inquiry must be an objective one: "the question is whether the officer's actions are 'objectively reasonable' in light of the facts and circumstances confronting them, without regard to their underlying intent or motivation."[33] "An officer's evil intentions," the Court concluded, "will not make a Fourth Amendment violation out of an objectively reasonable use of force; nor will an officer's good intentions make an objectively unreasonable use of force constitutional."[34] This last interpretive rule adheres to the traditional Fourth Amendment principle that an officer's subjective intent will not invalidate otherwise lawful conduct.[35]

Based on *Garner* and *Graham*, lower courts consistently applied the following tests: if deadly force was used, the court would assess whether the suspect posed a threat to the safety of the officers or others; if non-deadly force was used, a reviewing court would assess the three factors from *Graham*. However, in the 2007 case *Scott v. Harris*, the Court rejected these multi-factor tests and reiterated that the Fourth Amendment's more general free-form reasonableness test should apply.[36]

Scott v. Harris's Free-Form Approach

In *Scott*, the officers concluded a high-speed car chase by ramming the back of the suspect's bumper with a police cruiser, sending the suspect off the road, where he crashed and was rendered a quadriplegic.[37] Bringing a Section 1983 claim, the plaintiff argued that because the police technique constituted deadly force that *Garner* should control the analysis. Rejecting this approach, Justice Scalia, writing for an 8-1 Court, observed that "*Garner* did not establish a magical on/off switch that triggers rigid preconditions whenever an officer's actions constitute 'deadly force.' *Garner* was simply an application of the Fourth Amendment's 'reasonableness' test to the use of a particular type of force in a particular situation."[38]

In his analysis, Justice Scalia surprisingly did not cite to *Graham* or the three *Graham* factors, and instructed that courts must instead "slosh [their] way through the factbound morass of 'reasonableness.'"[39] The *Scott* Court did note, however, that one factor to take into consideration was the relative culpabilities of the suspect and innocent bystanders. Weighing the totality of the circumstances, the Court ultimately held that "[a] police officer's attempt to terminate a dangerous high-speed car chase that threatens the lives of innocent bystanders does not violate the Fourth Amendment, even when it places the fleeing motorist at risk of serious injury or death."[40]

Some have come to criticize the *Scott* ruling as overly "simplistic" and have argued that it fails to provide appropriate guidance for future use of force cases.[41] Specifically, the ruling might not give officers in the field sufficient instruction on what level of force is reasonable in a particular situation. As one commentator noted, *Scott* "may serve as an incentive for agencies to re-write their policies in more general terms, avoiding specific preconditions for the use of deadly force."[42] This could potentially deprive officers of much needed instruction when in the field. The *Scott* ruling could also deprive juries of adequate instruction on what constitutes excessive force. As one post-*Scott* district court has noted:

> [D]eadly force is simply a type of excessive force. No separate legal standard applies to cases involving deadly force. Like any other excessive force claim, cases involving deadly or potentially deadly force should be evaluated under the *Graham* reasonableness test. Here, as in *Scott*, the Court has no need to decide as a matter of law whether the police used deadly force. Accordingly, the Court need only craft a charge which will help a jury decide whether the force used in this case was reasonable under all the circumstances.... The Court will not instruct the jury as to the definition of deadly force or the specific circumstances under which deadly force is or is not reasonable.[43]

As the Eighth Circuit noted in a pre-*Scott* case, failing to adequately explain the difference between deadly and non-deadly force could confuse juries:

> The problem with giving only the more general excessive-force instruction is that it may mislead the jury as to what is permissible under the law. One can easily imagine a jury, having been given only the general standard, concluding that an officer was "objectively reasonable" in shooting a fleeing suspect who posed no threat to the officer or others.[44]

As will be discussed in the next section, lower courts have interpreted this line of excessive force cases in divergent ways: some still rely on the multifactor tests of *Garner* and *Graham*, while others have held that *Scott*'s free-form test should control.

Assessing the Use of Excessive Force

Based upon Supreme Court case law, the following rules apply to an assessment of excessive use of force:

- All claims of excessive force occurring in the course of an arrest, investigatory stop, or other seizure are
- reviewed under the Fourth Amendment's prohibition against unreasonable seizures.
- An officer's use of force must be "objectively reasonable" under the totality of the circumstances.
- Reasonableness is determined by balancing the interests of the individual and the government.
- Reasonableness is evaluated from the perspective of a reasonable officer in the field.

Deadly Force

One of the most prominent issues surrounding police use of force has been use of deadly force against unarmed suspects. Some have raised concerns that officers are resorting to deadly force too quickly or without sufficient justification.

Although police use of deadly force, like all uses of force, is a fact-intensive inquiry that depends on the specifics of each particular case, a few trends can be noted. First, police are generally permitted to employ deadly force when the suspect is carrying a deadly weapon in what is perceived by the officer to be a threatening manner. For example, in *Montoute v. Carr*, the Eleventh Circuit held that the suspect's possession of a sawed-off shotgun posed a risk of serious physical harm to the officer or others, justifying the use of deadly force.[45] Similarly, the Fourth Circuit in the 2013 case *Ayala v. Wolfe* upheld the deadly use of force against a robbery suspect who pulled a firearm from his waistband as he was being frisked by police.[46]

Second, even where a suspect turns out to not have a firearm, the courts have held that officers are still justified in using deadly force if they reasonably believed the suspect was carrying a gun.[47] For instance, the Eleventh Circuit upheld the use of force against a fleeing suspect who had just physically assaulted an officer and appeared to be reaching under his seat for an undisclosed object, although no weapon was found in the car after the incident.[48] In another case, the Fourth Circuit upheld the shooting of a man believed to be reaching for a firearm, but which turned out to be a can of shoe polish, even though the only evidence of such possession was a citizen's report of it, corroborated by the officer's own observation.[49]

Third, the courts have generally been unwilling to second-guess officers in the field and will approve the use of force in wide-ranging contexts. Indeed, one federal court noted that "[t]his standard contains a built-in measure of deference to the officer's on-the-spot judgment about the level of force necessary in light of the circumstances of the particular case."[50] This deference results in rules such as the one that officers are not required to use less intrusive force if the use of force in question was reasonable under the Fourth Amendment.[51] In upholding this rule, the Ninth Circuit argued "'[r]equiring officers to find and choose the least intrusive alternative would require them to exercise superhuman judgment" and could "induce tentativeness" in officers that might deter them from protecting the public and themselves.[52] However, some courts have noted that the "availability of alternative means" is "relevant" to a Fourth Amendment analysis.[53]

Although significant deference is accorded officers, possession of a weapon does not always justify police use of deadly force. Take, for example, the 2013 Fourth Circuit case *Cooper v. Sheehan*.[54] There, the court held that it is the *threat* posed by the possession of a firearm that justifies the use of force, not the mere possession of a firearm.[55] The court concluded that Cooper did not pose such a threat—he was coming out of his home, held the gun towards the ground, made no sudden moves, made no threats, and did not ignore any commands.[56]

Fourth, there is divergence in the lower courts in applying the Supreme Court's limited deadly force jurisprudence. For instance, questions remain whether courts should still be giving Garner's deadly force instructions after *Scott* instructed that reasonableness is the touchstone of assessing excessive force claims. Likewise, it is unclear after *Scott* how the three *Graham* factors play into the analysis. Based on Justice Scalia's rejection of *Garner* as controlling all excessive force cases, his failure to even cite to *Graham*, and admonishment that courts must still "slosh [their] way through the factbound morass of reasonableness," it appears that courts must assess excessive force claims under a free-form totality of the circumstances evaluation, untethered from *Garner* and *Graham*.[57]

Since *Scott*, several circuits, including the Ninth and Eleventh circuits, have applied this freeform approach. In *Mattos v. Agaronos*, the Ninth Circuit noted that the *Graham* factors "are not exclusive" and that courts must "examine the totality of the circumstances and consider whatever specific factors may be appropriate in a particular case, whether or not listed in *Graham*."[58] Similarly, the Eleventh Circuit observed that "none of [the *Garner*] conditions are prerequisites to the lawful application of deadly force by an officer seizing a suspect."[59]

Other circuits, on the other hand, including the Second,[60] Fourth,[61] Fifth,[62] and Sixth[63] have failed to apply *Scott*'s more general inquiry. In *Rasanen v. Doe*, for instance, the district court provided a jury instruction that failed to include the justifications for use of deadly force provided in *Garner*, but instead provided a general reasonableness instruction.[64] On appeal, the Second Circuit asserted that although *Scott* "clarified that a special instruction based on *Garner* is not necessary (or even appropriate) in all deadly-force contexts," a *Garner* instruction should still be given in its original context: "the fatal shooting of an unarmed suspect."[65] Thus, in the Second Circuit, in a case "involving use of force highly likely to have deadly effects, an instruction regarding justifications for the use of deadly force is required."[66]

Non-Deadly Force

Like the use of deadly force, use of so-called "non-deadly," "non-lethal," or "less than lethal" force has caused controversy in recent months. Although nominally non-lethal, recent deaths caused by chokeholds,[67] tasers,[68] and pepper spray[69] have raised significant concerns about when these methods of force should be permitted. Moreover, some in the public have questioned the use of pepper spray, batons, and other non-lethal uses of force against individuals who are protesting the very use of force being used against them.[70]

Tasers

Over the past several decades, law enforcement agencies in the United States have significantly increased their acquisition of tasers—a weapon capable of incapacitating a human being with an electroshock.[71] As of 2013, over 12,000 law enforcement agencies were reportedly using tasers.[72] While apparently reducing the numbers of police shootings and held out as a safer alternative to the use of a firearm, it has been reported that between 2001 and 2012, 500 people died after being shocked with a taser.[73]

Tasers can be deployed in two modes. One of the most popular tasers used in the field—the X26, made by Taser International, Inc.—can fire two probes up to 35 feet and "discharges pulsed energy to deliver a 50,000 volt shock designed to override the subject's central nervous system, causing uncontrollable contraction of the muscle tissue and instant collapse."[74] Alternatively, the X26 and other similar devices can be used in "stun mode," in which the device is physically pressed against a human body to deliver a more localized shock.[75]

Like all other use of force cases, those assessing the use of tasers tend to be heavily fact-specific from which it is difficult to derive universal principles. That said, a few general trends can be noted. First, the courts have held that the use of a taser is least justified against "nonviolent misdemeanants who do not flee or actively resist arrest and pose little or no threat to the security of the officer."[76] For instance, in *Brown v. City of Golden Valley*, a woman and her husband were allegedly pulled over for speeding.[77] When the officers reportedly engaged in aggressive behavior, the woman called 911, and refused to hang up when commanded by the officers.[78] One of the officers tased her arm and threw the phone on the ground. The Eighth Circuit rejected the officer's defense of qualified immunity, noting that the woman was only suspected of committing a minor offense and did not pose a threat to the safety of the officers.[79] In another case, the Sixth Circuit held that an officer was not entitled to qualified immunity when she "gratuitously" shocked a man after he had been restrained by police.[80]

Second, the courts have generally held that the use of a taser against persons who are belligerent or violent is permitted under the Fourth Amendment.[81] In one case, a 9th grade student was tased by a police officer after he attempted to punch a police officer after refusing to hand over his portable video game console.[82] The court rejected the student's Section 1983 claim, observing that it was "simply impossible" to say that the amount of force used was unreasonable under the Fourth Amendment.

Somewhere in the grey area between active resistance and no resistance are cases where law enforcement used a taser against someone who was *passively* resisting the officer's commands. The majority of cases seem to permit the use of a taser for individuals against such passive resisters. In *Buckley v. Haddock*, for example, the Eleventh Circuit upheld the use of a taser on a man who fell to the ground after being handcuffed and refused to get up after several requests from the officer.[83] After giving the man several warnings, the officer tased him several times. In rejecting his claim, the court put significant weight on the government's interest, noting that "[t]he government has an interest in arrests being completed efficiently and without waste of limited resources: police time and energy that may be needed elsewhere at any moment."[84]

In another case, the U.S. District Court for the Southern District of Ohio held that a police officer was justified in using a taser on an elderly suspect suffering from Alzheimer's disease who had "refused to comply" with the officer's orders. Once the officer decided to engage the suspect, the court posited, "he had to continue, and it seems the only way he was able to do this was with a taser."[85] In doing so, the court denied the fact that the age or potential mental illness of a suspect should require a heightened use of force standard.[86]

Similarly, the Western District of Washington upheld the use of a taser against a mentally ill woman who attempted to drive away from two police officers who were sent to check on the suspect after her mother reported that she might attempt suicide.[87] The district court upheld this use of force for two reasons. First, it found credible the officer's belief that Lowe posed a risk to the safety of the officers and others when she got into her truck, which he believed could have been used as a weapon. Second, the court construed Lowe's actions as "attempting to avoid legitimate contact by law enforcement.... "[88]

Beyond the level of threat posed by the individual, the courts have taken other factors into consideration including the degree of harm caused by the Taser and how many times it was used in a specific situation.[89] For instance, the Eleventh Circuit observed that "[a]lthough being struck by a taser gun is an unpleasant experience, the amount of force [the officer] used—a single use of a taser gun causing a one-time shocking—was reasonably proportionate to the need for force and did not inflict any serious injury."[90] To the contrary, the fact that an individual had suffered "serious injury requiring emergency medical care" and its multiple applications contributed to a court finding that the use of a taser multiple times was unreasonable.[91] Because in the large majority of cases the target of the tasing is not going to suffer permanent injuries, the courts may be inclined to find that such use of force is reasonable in most cases. However, these opinions did not take into account the potential injury—including death—that might be caused by these devices. Other factors taken into consideration have included the vulnerability of the victim,[92] and whether the officers provided a warning to the target before employing the taser.[93]

Pepper Spray

Like tasers, the use of pepper spray by local police as a law enforcement tool has engendered considerable public attention, including well-known incidents during the Occupy Wall Street protests,[94] and more recently during the protests in Ferguson, Missouri.[95]

Pepper spray, or "oleoresin capsicum ("OC"), is a chemical agent used by law enforcement to subdue violent or combative suspects without resorting to higher levels of force.[96] The effects of pepper spray include "(1) dilation of the capillaries and instant closing of the eyes through swelling of the eyelids, (2) immediate respiratory inflammation, including uncontrollable coughing, retching, shortness of breath and gasping for air with a gagging sensation in the throat, and (3) immediate burning sensations to the mucous membranes, skin and inside the nose and mouth."[97]

The federal courts have generally been less deferential to law enforcement when using pepper spray on passive resisters than they have been with tasers. In cases in which the individual is only passively resisting—say, simply failing to listen to an officer's order—the courts have generally held that the use of pepper spray is a violation of the Fourth Amendment.[98] Take, for instance, *Young v. County of Los Angeles*, in which the Ninth Circuit held that the use of pepper spray against a nonviolent traffic offender was unreasonable under the Fourth Amendment.[99] Similarly, in *Headwaters Forest Defense v. County of Humboldt*, the Ninth Circuit held that the use of pepper spray against nonviolent protestors constituted an unreasonable seizure under the Fourth Amendment.[100]

While these cases disapproved of the use of pepper spray against persons who were passive resisters, there have been rulings upholding such use of force in the course of traffic stops. In *Mecham v. Frazier*, the Tenth Circuit rejected the plaintiff's Fourth Amendment claim that a police officer used excessive force when he sprayed her with pepper spray after she refused to leave her vehicle after a traffic stop.[101] The court found that the officer's actions were justified based on Mecham's "disregard for the officer's instructions, the length of the encounter, and the implausibility of Mecham's rationale for not cooperating." Like the use of tasers, the courts have generally held that an officer's use of pepper spray is not unreasonable when a suspect is actively resisting arrest or fails to heed an officer's direct command. In *Singleton v. Darby*, the Fifth Circuit upheld the use of pepper spray against a group of individuals, including the plaintiff Jeanette Singleton, who were protesting the Keystone XL Pipeline.[102] In rejecting Singleton's Section 1983 claim premised on excessive force, the court held that the use of the pepper spray was not unreasonable because (1) the state had a significant interest in keeping public roads clear; (2) the officer faced an "explosive situation" in which he was greatly outnumbered by the protesters; (3) he provided a warning before using the spray; and (4) pepper spray was likely the least intrusive force available to the officer.[103]

Finally, like with tasers, federal courts have generally held that it is unreasonable to use pepper spray against individuals who are not resisting and pose no danger to the officer or others.[104]

Assessing the Reasonableness of Non-Deadly Force

Based on federal case law, the following questions have been asked when assessing the reasonableness of the non-deadly use of force:

- Was the individual actively or passively resisting arrest or capture?
- What was the severity of the crime?
- Was the individual in a class of vulnerable persons (e.g., mental disability, age)?
- What was the extent, if any, of the individual's injuries inflicted by the use of force?
- How many times, for how long, and where on the individual's body was the force employed?
- Did the officer provide a warning?

REMEDIES FOR USE OF FORCE

To provide legal remedies for the unconstitutional use of force by law enforcement officers, Congress has primarily relied on three federal statutes: (1) a criminal offense for violations of constitutional rights, including excessive force; (2) a civil cause of action for deprivation of such rights; and (3) a statute authorizing the Attorney General to bring civil suits for injunctive relief against police departments engaged in a "pattern or practice" of such unconstitutional use of force. In each of these statutes, Congress relied on its power under the Fourteenth Amendment to "enforce, by appropriate legislation" certain constitutional safeguards including the right to be free from unreasonable seizures.[105]

Federal Criminal Civil Rights Statute (18 U.S.C. § 242)

Following the Civil War, Congress enacted the Civil Rights Act of 1866, which made it a criminal offense to deprive another of a civil right while acting under color of law. While primarily intending to protect the rights of newly freed African Americans, the statute protects victims of all races.[106] Codified at 18 U.S.C. § 242, the statute provides, in relevant part,

> Whoever, under color of any law, statute, ordinance, regulation, or custom, willfully subjects any person in any State, Territory, Commonwealth, Possession, or District to the deprivation of any rights, privileges, or immunities secured or protected by the Constitution or laws of the United States, or to different punishments, pains, or penalties, on account of such person being an alien, or by reason of his color, or race, than are prescribed for the punishment of citizens, shall be fined under this title or imprisoned not more than one year, or both[.][107]

A prosecution under Section 242 requires the government to prove three elements: (1) the defendant deprived an individual of a right secured by the Constitution or the laws of the United States; (2) he or she acted under color of law when depriving this individual of constitutional right; and (3) acted willfully to deprive such individual of this right. Again, prosecutions under Section 242 do not require that the officer use force based upon an individual's race.[108] It is enough that the individual is deprived of his or her constitutional rights.

For various reasons, including sympathetic juries, the close relationship between the police and prosecutors, the high evidentiary threshold needed to secure a conviction, and lack of resources, Section 242 is not frequently utilized.[109] In fact, it has been reported that between 1981 and 1990, DOJ only prosecuted 1% of civil rights complaints it received.[110]

Perhaps the greatest hurdle to successful prosecutions under Section 242 is its specific intent element.[111] As originally drafted, the statute did not require that a constitutional deprivation be done "willfully";[112] however, Congress added that term to the precursor to Section 242 as part of the criminal code codification in 1909,[113] evidently in an attempt to make the section "less severe."[114] DOJ has declined to prosecute Section 242 cases at an extremely high rate, with "lack of criminal intent" being one of the primary reasons.[115] To understand why prosecutions might be so limited and what Congress might do, if anything, to alter the current statute, the seminal 1945 Supreme Court case *United States v. Screws* and subsequent federal circuit court cases interpreting Section 242's *mens rea* requirement must be reviewed.

Screws v. United States and the Specific Intent Requirement

In *Screws*, the Court faced a "shocking and revolting episode in law enforcement."[116] In that case, M. Claude Screws, Sheriff of Baker County, Georgia; Frank Jones, a police officer; and Jim Kelley, a special deputy, went late at night to Robert Hall's home to arrest him for theft of a tire.[117] Hall, a 30-year-old African American, was handcuffed and taken by car to the courthouse. Upon arriving at the courthouse, the three officers began beating him with their fists and with a "solid-bar blackjack about eight inches long and weighing two pounds."[118] They claimed that Hall had attempted to pull out a gun and had used insulting language towards the officers. After Young, still handcuffed, had been knocked to the ground, the officers beat him mercilessly from 15 to 30 minutes until he was unconscious. Hall's body was then dragged feet first through the courthouse yard into the jail and "thrown upon the floor dying."[119] He was taken to the hospital, but died less than an hour later without ever regaining consciousness. The three officers were charged under 18 U.S.C. § 52—the precursor to Section 242.

The prosecution was premised on the claim that the officers deprived Hall of "life without due process of law."[120] The defendants challenged the statute on vagueness grounds, arguing that they were being prosecuted under a constitutional provision that "provides no ascertainable standard of guilt."[121] Justice Douglas, writing for a four-member plurality joined by Chief Justice Stone and Justices Black and Reed, attempted to assuage such concerns by noting that "the decisions of the courts are ... a source of reference for ascertaining the specific concept of due process." At the same time, Justice Douglas acknowledged that the act "incorporate[d] by reference a large body of changing and uncertain law" that could "cast law enforcement agencies loose at their own risk on a vast uncharted sea."[122] To remedy this potential vagueness problem, Justice Douglas turned to the interpretation of the *mens rea* element.

Justice Douglas noted that traditionally the *mens rea* term "intent" only required that "if a man intentionally adopts certain conduct in certain circumstances, he intentionally breaks the law in the only sense in which the law ever considers intent."[123] However, the plurality noted that merely requiring this form of general intent would make government actors into criminals "though his motive was pure and his purpose was unrelated to the disregard of any constitutional guarantee."[124] Latching onto the term "willfully" in the statute, the plurality noted that generally "willfully" means "an act done with bad purpose," and, as such, "an evil motive to accomplish that which the statute condemns becomes a constituent element of the crime."[125] Requiring proof of a "specific intent to do a prohibited act may avoid those consequences to the accused which may otherwise render a vague or indefinite statute invalid."[126] The thinking goes, if a person specifically intends to violate the constitutional rights of another, he cannot then complain he did not know what he was doing violated the law.

In an effort to further explain this standard, the plurality infused confusion into its new rule. First, the Court noted that the defendant need not "have been thinking in constitutional terms ... where their aim was not to enforce local law but to deprive a citizen of a right and that right was protected by the Constitution."[127] As noted by one circuit court, there seems to be some contradiction in saying that the officers need not be thinking in constitutional terms, but that it is enough that their "aim" is to deprive a citizen of a constitutional right.[128] How can an officer aim to deprive a citizen of a right if he or she is not thinking in terms of that right?[129] The Court does not provide a clear answer.

Second, although he asserted that specific intent is required under Section 242, Justice Douglas then posited that an individual can be prosecuted under the lesser "reckless disregard" *mens rea* standard: "[A defendant] is under no necessity of guessing whether the statute applies to him for he either knows or acts in reckless disregard of its prohibition of the deprivation of a defined constitutional or other federal right."[130] The plurality similarly noted in another part of the opinion: "When they act willfully in the sense in which we use the word, they act in open defiance or in reckless disregard of a constitutional requirement which has been made specific and definite."[131]

Needless to say, *Screws* "is not a model of clarity."[132] On the one hand, it seemed to be saying that requiring specific intent was necessary to ensure that the statute was not unnecessarily vague. On the other hand, the plurality opinion appeared to endorse a "reckless disregard" standard—a *mens rea* standard significantly lower than specific intent and one that would likely permit many more prosecutions to go forward.

Circuit Courts' Interpretation of Section 242

In the wake of *Screws*, the lower courts have been left to determine the meaning of "willfully" and how to apply Section 242's specific intent requirement. In one camp, several courts read *Screws* and Section 242 stringently to require that a defendant have the specific intent to do what the law forbids. In another camp, courts seem to require an intent to do the physical act, but not necessarily the purpose to violate another's constitutionally protected right, akin to general intent at common law. In the third group, courts have latched onto the "reckless disregard" language from the plurality opinion in *Screws* to permit a conviction under Section 242 on this lesser *mens rea* standard.

Courts in the first camp have read *Screws* strictly to require not only an intent to commit the physical act in question, but also an intent to deprive that person of a constitutional right. In *United States v. Garza*, a county sheriff in Texas and his special investigator were convicted under Section 242 for, among other things, arresting individuals without probable cause, detaining them for long periods, subjecting them to repeated questioning, and failing to bring them before a magistrate judge as required under Texas law.[133] At their trial, the district court defined "willfully" in Section 242 as follows:

> The word "willfully," as that term has been used from time to time in these instructions means that the act was committed voluntarily and purposely with the specific intent to do something the law forbids. That is to say, with a bad purpose either to disobey or to disregard the law.[134]

The Fifth Circuit upheld these instructions, finding that they complied with the Supreme Court's instructions that "willfully in 18 U.S.C. § 242 implies conscious purpose to do wrong and intent to deprive another of a right guaranteed by the Constitution, federal statutes, or decisional law."[135] Indeed, this instruction seems to comport with the more stringent rule announced in *Screws* that the defendant must actually intend to violate the constitutional rights of the victim.

In an earlier case, *United States v. Kelsey*, the Fifth Circuit reversed the defendant's conviction based upon the district court's failure to properly instruct the jury on the "willfully" element under Section 242.[136] There, the district court had instructed the jury as follows:

> [T]he evidence must establish beyond reasonable doubt that the Defendant knew that the degree of force which he utilized on Mr. de la Osa at the time of the arrest was not reasonably necessary to effect the arrest, but, despite this knowledge, he knowingly and intentionally exerted force which he knew to be unlawful under all the circumstances to accomplish the arrest.
>
> An act is done "intentionally" if it is done voluntarily and with the specific intent to do the act in question, as distinguished from an act done

through inadvertence, mistake, accident or for some other innocent reason.[137]

The Fifth Circuit rejected the district court's instructions for two reasons. First, although the district court instructed the jury that the defendant had to knowingly and intentionally exert force that he knew to be unlawful, it did not "instruct the jury that willfulness means an act which is done with a bad purpose or an evil motive."[138] Second, although the instruction required that the act be done with the specific intent to do the act in question, it failed to require that he have the specific intent to deprive the victim of his constitutional rights.[139] Thus, under the Fifth Circuit's test, it is not enough that the defendant intentionally and knowingly commits an act which he *knows* would violate an individual's rights; he must *intend* to violate those rights.

Similarly, the Northern District of Ohio applied this more stringent test in a case stemming from the National Guard shooting at Kent State. There, the court held that

> even the specific intent to injure, or the reckless use of excessive force, without more, does not satisfy the requirements of § 242 as construed in *Screws*. There must exist an intention to 'punish or to prevent the exercise of constitutionally guaranteed rights, such as the right to vote, or to obtain equal protection of the law.'[140]

The second group of courts permits a somewhat lesser showing by requiring that the defendant intend to commit the physical act, but not necessarily intend to violate the constitutional rights of another. In *United States v. Cobb*, the Fourth Circuit addressed an appeal by three officers who were convicted under Section 242 for beating a prisoner while detained and in handcuffs.[141] At the trial, the district court provided the following instruction on the *mens rea* element of Section 242:

> Fourth, that the defendant willfully and knowingly intended to subject Kenneth Pack to the deprivation of his constitutionally protected right....
>
> [The government] must show that a defendant had the specific intent to deprive Kenneth Pack of his right not to be subjected to unreasonable and excessive force. If you find that a defendant knew what he was doing and that he intended to do what he was doing, and if you find that he did violate a constitutional right, then you may conclude that the defendant

acted with the specific intent to deprive the victim of that constitutional right.[142]

In its brief analysis, the Fourth Circuit upheld this instruction, observing that "the instruction on element (4) expressly conditions guilt on a finding that the defendants 'willfully and knowingly' acted with a 'specific intent to deprive' Pack of his liberty interest." The court continued: "The instruction could not have been more emphatic that conviction was contingent upon a finding that appellants wilfully, knowingly, and intentionally assaulted Pack in contravention of his constitutional rights."[143] It appears from this language that the court did not require that the defendant intentionally violate the rights of another, but instead that he intended to engage in the physical act. Again, in *Screws*, Justice Douglas noted that *traditionally* "intent" only required that "if a man intentionally adopts certain conduct in certain circumstances, he intentionally breaks the law in the only sense in which the law ever considers intent." This is one iteration of what was known as general intent at common law. However, Justice Douglas went on to say in *Screws* that under Section 242 this form of general intent was insufficient. It appears that the Fourth Circuit was adopting this form of general intent rejected by the plurality in *Screws*. That said, in *Screws*, the court also endorsed a reckless disregard standard that is lower than both specific intent and general intent.

Courts in the third camp require the least stringent showing under Section 242 by permitting a conviction under a reckless disregard standard. The Third Circuit adopted this approach after conceding that it had great difficulty in reconciling the seemingly inconsistent statements in *Screws*.[144] In an attempt to reconcile these "facially inconsistent standards—that an individual can intend to violate a right even if the individual is not thinking in terms of any right," the court accepted that willfulness in Section 242 can include reckless disregard. The only remaining question for the court was whether this standard should be applied subjectively or objectively.[145] An objective standard, generally used in the civil context, would require that the officer was indifferent to the rights of another that the officer knew or was so obvious that the officer should have known.[146] The subjective standard, on the other hand, would require that the prosecution prove that the defendant was indifferent to a right that he was personally aware, either through training or otherwise.[147] The Third Circuit did not resolve this question, as it found that the officer was liable under either standard.[148]

The Ninth Circuit in *United States v. Gwaltney* similarly upheld the following reckless disregard instruction: "It is not necessary for the government to prove the defendant was thinking in constitutional terms at the time of the incident, for a reckless disregard for a person's constitutional rights is evidence of specific intent to deprive that person of those rights."[149]

In sum, there is much debate in the lower courts about how exactly to interpret the phrase "willfully" in Section 242 or how to apply the *Screws* ruling. Confusion in the lower courts in such a sensitive area of the law could be considered troublesome for two reasons. First, the subject matter—the use of deadly force—is the most serious action a government can take against its citizenry. Second, with a potential penalty of life imprisonment or death, it would be beneficial to officers in the field to know exactly what level of culpability is required to subject them to these punishments.

The recent shootings in Ferguson and elsewhere have prompted some commentators to call for an overhaul of Section 242 to better clarify the *mens rea* element in the hopes of spurring more consistent enforcement.[150] In its 2000 report "Revisiting *Who is Guarding the Guardians*," the U.S. Commission on Civil Rights recommended removing the specific intent standard.[151] However, as discussed, the Third and Ninth Circuits already employ a reckless disregard standard, but it is not clear whether this less stringent burden of proof has prompted DOJ to bring more prosecutions in those circuits.

Additionally, there could be unintended consequences to lowering the *mens rea* threshold in Section 242. If Section 242 is amended, it will affect not only cases of excessive force, but all claims of constitutional violations by those acting under color of law. This might work to ensnare the unknowing government worker that unwittingly violates the constitutional rights of another. For example, the town clerk who denies a parade permit might be deemed to recklessly disregard the First Amendment rights of an applicant. A more targeted approach would be to create a standalone statute that lowers the mens rea specifically for police use of force cases. This is well within Congress's authority, as it had the constitutional authority to pass Section 242 to begin with, and this standalone statute would merely represent a part of that subject matter.

No matter which *mens rea* standard is used, Section 242 is a *criminal* statute, and as such the prosecution must still prove beyond a reasonable doubt that the government official committed the offense.[152] Civil suits under the federal civil rights statute, on the other hand, require a lower threshold—preponderance of the evidence—and have had much greater success in the courtroom.

Federal Civil Rights Claims (42 U.S.C. § 1983)

In addition to criminal liability, victims of police abuse can bring civil suits under 42 U.S.C. § 1983. Like Section 242, Section 1983 was enacted during the Reconstruction Era to secure the constitutional rights of African Americans.[153] Section 1983 provides, in relevant part:

> Every person who, under color of any statute, ordinance, regulation, custom, or usage, of any State or Territory or the District of Columbia, subjects, or causes to be subjected, any citizen of the United States or other person within the jurisdiction thereof to the deprivation of any rights, privileges, or immunities secured by the Constitution and laws, shall be liable to the party injured in an action at law, suit in equity, or other proper proceeding for redress[.][154]

Section 1983 "is not itself a source of substantive rights," but instead looks to the Fourth Amendment and other constitutional and civil rights laws for its content.[155] To prove a violation under Section 1983 for claims of excessive force, the plaintiff must prove that (1) the officer deprived the individual of his or her right to be free from unreasonable seizures under the Fourth Amendment and (2) the officer acted under color of law.[156] Note that Section 1983, "unlike its criminal counterpart, 18 U.S.C. § 242, contains no state-of-mind requirement independent of that necessary to state a violation of the underlying constitutional right."[157] Plaintiffs in Section 1983 actions can seek damages, injunctive relief, or other equitable relief.[158]

Qualified Immunity

Even if an officer has engaged in unconstitutional conduct, the doctrine of qualified immunity insulates an officer from personal civil liability if his or her actions did not "violate clearly established statutory or constitutional rights of which a reasonable person would have known."[159] The Court has noted that qualified immunity represents a balance between two important interests: "the need to hold public officials accountable when they exercise power irresponsibly and the need to shield officials from harassment, distraction, and liability when they perform their duties reasonably."[160] That qualified immunity provides a broad shield to liability is evidenced by the Court's observation that it "provides ample protection to all but the plainly incompetent or those who knowingly violate the law."[161] This doctrine has frequently come under attack for shielding officers from liability even when they have engaged in unconstitutional conduct.[162] In response to this concern, it should be noted that qualified immunity appears to be derived from common law, and is not constitutionally compelled. Thus, Congress can alter its contours or eliminate it altogether via statute.

The process for applying this doctrine has evolved in recent years. Under older precedent, the Court mandated a two-step sequence for qualified immunity claims.[163] First, a reviewing court had to decide whether the facts alleged by the plaintiff amounted to a constitutional violation.

Second, if the plaintiff made this showing, the court had to decide whether the right was "clearly established" at the time of the misconduct. The Court noted that skipping ahead to the "clearly established" prong of the test would deprive future courts of case law defining the parameters of the right in question. However, lower courts frequently criticized this "rigid order of battle" on "practical, procedural, and substantive grounds."[164] Under the older regime, lower courts were required to fully litigate the constitutional merits when in many instances it was obvious that the law relied upon was not clearly established at the time. In an effort to give courts more flexibility, in the 2009 case *Pearson v. Callahan*, the Court overruled its prior rule and held that lower courts "should be permitted to exercise their sound discretion in deciding which of the two prongs of the qualified immunity analysis should be addressed first in light of the circumstances in the particular case at hand."[165] That being said, the Court noted that following the *Saucier* order is "often beneficial."[166]

For a law to be clearly established, "the contours of the right must be sufficiently clear that a reasonable official would understand that what he is doing violates that right."[167] This provides officers "fair warning" which conduct will violate the Constitution.[168] This standard "depends substantially upon the level of generality at which the relevant 'legal rule' is to be identified."[169] The Court has instructed lower courts not to define a clearly established rule at a high level of generality.[170] That being said, the Court does "not require a case directly on point, but existing precedent must have placed the statutory or constitutional question beyond debate."[171]

In the use of force context, the major Supreme Court precedents, *Tennessee v. Garner*,[172] *Graham v. Connor*,[173] and *Scott v. Harris*,[174] are each written at a very high level of abstraction. As aptly noted by Justice Scalia, the very nature of the objective reasonableness/totality of the circumstances approach necessarily requires courts to "slosh [their] way through the factbound morass of 'reasonableness.'"[175] The by-product of the generality of these tests is that they commonly cannot be applied as precedents in use of force qualified immunity cases. For instance, in *Wilson v. City of Lafayette*, the Tenth Circuit addressed the use of a taser that resulted in the death of the suspect.[176] After concluding that there were no controlling circuit cases on point at the time (2006), the court looked to Supreme Court case law but found that there was no "clear lesson to be drawn from *Graham*," and thus granted the officer qualified immunity.

Note that even if an officer is held liable under Section 1983 in his personal capacity, he may be indemnified by state or local government.[177] The right to indemnification is not governed by federal law, but is a matter of state or local law.

Municipal Liability

In addition to suing the police officers directly involved in an incident of excessive force, many Section 1983 plaintiffs can go after the "deep pocket of municipalities" that employ these officers.[178] In a series of cases, the Court addressed under what circumstances municipalities may be held liable under Section 1983.

The Court in *Monell v. Department of Social Services of New York* held that municipalities can be held liable as "persons" under Section 1983, but only when the municipality *itself* caused the constitutional violation.[179] Thus, a municipality cannot be held liable solely because it employs someone who violates the constitutional rights of another.[180] Rather, to hold a municipality liable, it must be the execution of the government's "policy or custom" that inflicts the constitutional injury.[181]

In *City of Canton, Ohio v. Harris*, the Court addressed whether a failure to train can rise to the level of a "policy." The Court answered in the affirmative, but limited this rule to instances where the failure to train amounted to a "deliberate indifference to the rights of persons with whom the police come into contact."[182] A failure to adequately train a class of officers will not always be deemed a city "policy." It is only where the "need for more training is so obvious, and the inadequacy so likely to result in the violation of constitutional rights, that the policymakers of the city can be said to have been deliberately indifferent to the need."[183]

In *Board of County Commissioners of Bryan Country v. Brown*, the Court addressed whether a single hiring decision by a municipality can be a "policy" permitting *Monell* liability.[184] In that case, the plaintiff was severely injured after she was thrown to the ground during a traffic stop by a sheriff's deputy with a criminal history, including arrests for assault and battery, resisting arrest, and public drunkenness. The plaintiff proceeded against the county on the theory that its hiring decision resulted in her injury. Although the Court did not foreclose the theory that one hiring decision might result in liability, it observed that "rigorous standards of culpability and causation must be applied to ensure that the municipality is not held liable solely for the actions of its employee."[185] Ultimately, the Court rejected the plaintiff's claim, noting that she had not demonstrated that the sheriff's hiring decision reflected a "conscious disregard for a high risk" that the officer would use excessive force in violation of the plaintiff's constitutional rights.[186]

"Pattern or Practice" Suits (42 U.S.C. § 14141)

The third federal remedy for unconstitutional conduct by law enforcement officers is 42 U.S.C. § 14141, the "pattern or practice" statute. Enacted as part of the Violent Crime Control and Law Enforcement Act of 1994, the need for this statute was partially prompted by several judicial rulings that held that both private litigants and the Department of Justice (DOJ) lacked legal standing to seek equitable relief to stop unlawful police practices absent specific statutory authorization.[187]

Section 14141 prohibits government authorities or agents acting on their behalf from engaging in a "pattern or practice of conduct by law enforcement officers ... that deprives persons of rights ... secured or protected by the Constitution or laws of the United States."[188] It authorizes the Attorney General to sue for equitable or declaratory relief when he or she has "reasonable cause to believe" that such a pattern of constitutional violation has occurred.

The scope of investigations under Section 14141, primarily conducted by the Special Litigation Section of DOJ's Civil Rights Division, has ranged from police use of force and unlawful stops and searches to racial and ethnic biases.[189] Many of these investigations are resolved by consent decree—a judicially enforceable settlement between DOJ and the local police department—which outlines the various measures the local agency must take to remedy its unconstitutional police practices. For instance, after two years of extensive investigation into the New Orleans Police Department's policies and practices in which DOJ found numerous instances of unconstitutional conduct, DOJ entered into a consent decree with the City of New Orleans requiring the city to implement new policies and training to remedy these constitutional violations.[190] The content of each consent decree can differ, but many include provisions concerning use-of-force reporting systems, citizen complaint systems, and early warning systems to identify problem officers.[191]

REFORMING POLICE USE OF FORCE

In response to the recent law enforcement-related deaths in Ferguson and elsewhere, Members have introduced various bills in the 114th Congress to rein in police use of excessive force and provide accountability.

Excessive Use of Force Prevention Act of 2015 (H.R. 2052)

The Excessive Use of Force Prevention Act of 2015 (H.R. 2052) would amend 18 U.S.C. § 242 so that "the application of any pressure to the throat or windpipe which may prevent or hinder breathing or reduce intake of air" would be considered "a punishment, pain, or penalty."[192] It is not clear how this statute would operate in practice. Most excessive force prosecutions brought under Section 242 rely on the statute's first prong, the deprivation of a constitutional right, and not the second prong, the unequal punishment on account of a person's race, color, or alien status.[193] It would appear that prosecutions under H.R. 2052 would occur only when an officer administers a chokehold as a punishment or penalty based on the suspect's race, color, or alien status.

Police Accountability Act of 2015 (H.R. 1102)

The Police Accountability Act of 2015 (H.R. 1101) would create a new federal crime for certain homicides committed by law enforcement officers.[194] H.R. 1102 would provide that any state or local officer in a public agency that receives funding under the Edward Byrne Memorial Justice Assistance Grant (JAG) Program who engages in conduct in the line of duty that would constitute murder or manslaughter if it were to occur in the special maritime and territorial jurisdiction of the United States would be punished as provided for that offense under federal law. The constitutionality of this bill has been addressed previously by CRS.[195]

National Statistics on Deadly Force Transparency Act of 2015 (H.R. 306)[196]

The National Statistics on Deadly Force Transparency Act of 2015 would reduce a state or local government's JAG funding[197] by 10% if it fails to submit data concerning police use of excessive force, including data concerning the following:

- identifying characteristics of the person who was the target of the use of deadly force and the officer who used deadly forced;
- time, date, and location of the use of deadly force;
- alleged criminal activity of the person who was the target of deadly force;
- nature of the deadly force used, including the use of a firearm;
- explanation, if any, from the relevant law enforcement agency on why deadly force was used;
- copy of deadly force guidelines in effect at the time deadly force was used; and
- description of any non-lethal efforts employed to apprehend or subdue the person who was the target of the use of deadly force before deadly force was used.

Police Reporting Information, Data and Evidence Act of 2015 (PRIDE Act) (S. 1476, H.R. 3481)

The Police Reporting Information, Data, and Evidence Act of 2015 (PRIDE Act) (S. 1476, H.R. 3481) would require the collection of data concerning any incident where the use of force by either a law enforcement officer or a civilian results in serious bodily injury or death. Such data shall include the following:

- gender, race, ethnicity, and age of each individual who was shot, injured, or killed;
- date, time, and location of the incident;
- whether the civilian was armed, and, if so, the type of weapon the civilian had;

- the type of force used against the officer, the civilian, or both, including the types of weapons used;
- number of officers involved in the incident; and
- a brief description regarding the circumstances surrounding the incident.

President's Task Force on 21st Century Policing

On December 21, 2014, President Barack Obama signed an executive order establishing the Task Force on 21st Century Policing.[198] The task force was charged with identifying best police practices, including use of force policies. In May 2015, the task force issued its final report with the following recommendations for law enforcement agencies concerning the use of force[199]

- Develop comprehensive policies on the use of force that include training, investigations, prosecutions, data collection, and information sharing. These policies must be clear, concise, and openly available for public inspection.
- Training on use of force should emphasize de-escalation and alternatives to arrest or summons in situations where appropriate.
- Mandate external and independent criminal investigations in cases of police use of force resulting in death, officer-involved shootings resulting in injury or death, or in-custody deaths.
- Mandate the use of external and independent prosecutors in cases of police use of force resulting in death, officer-involved shootings resulting in injury or death, or in-custody deaths.
- Require agencies to collect, maintain, and report data to the federal government on all officer-involved shootings, whether fatal or nonfatal, as well as any in-custody death.
- Policies should clearly state what types of information will be released, when, and in what situation, to maintain transparency.
- Establish a Serious Incident Review Board comprising sworn staff and community members to review cases involving officer-involved shootings and other serious incidents that have the potential to damage community trust or confidence in the agency. The purpose of this board should be to identify any administrative, supervisory, training, tactical, or policy issues that need to be addressed.

- Implement nonpunitive peer review of critical incidents separate from criminal and administrative investigations.

Other Reform Proposals

In addition to introduced legislation, academics, civil rights advocates, and others have suggested other reform proposals:

- lower the mens rea standard in 18 U.S.C. § 242;200
- create a standalone excessive force statute;201
- alter the "deliberate indifference" standard for failure to train claims under Section 1983;202 and
- amend 42 U.S.C. § 14141 to permit lawsuits by private citizens.203

End Notes

[1] Graham v. Connor, 490 U.S. 386, 396 (1989) ("Our Fourth Amendment jurisprudence has long recognized that the right to make an arrest or investigatory stop necessarily carries with it the right to use some degree of physical coercion or threat thereof to effect it.").

[2] Roberts v. Louisiana, 431 U.S. 633, 646-47 (1977) (Rehnquist, J., dissenting).

[3] Going hand-in-hand with this excessive force debate is the claim that state and local police forces have increasingly become "militarized" in their tactics and use of surplus military equipment from the Department of Defense, a practice recently ended by President Obama. See generally CRS Insight IN10138, The "Militarization" of Law Enforcement and the Department of Defense's "1033 Program", by Nathan James and Daniel H. Else.

[4] Angry Crowd Gathers after Missouri Police Shoot Teen, CBS NEWS (Aug. 10, 2014), available at http://www.cbsnews.com/news/angry-crowd-gathers-after-missouri-police-shoot-teen/; Ferguson Police Say Teen Shot by Cop Was Suspect in Robbery; Officer's Identity Revealed, CBS NEWS (Aug. 15, 2014, 9:47 A.M.), available at http://www.cbsnews.com/news/darren-wilson-ferguson-police-officer-who-fatally-shot-michael-brown-identified/.

[5] See, e.g., Elahe Izadi & Peter Holley, Video Shows Cleveland Officer Shooting 12-Year Old Tamir Rice Within Seconds, WASH. POST (Nov. 26, 2014), available at http://www.washingtonpost.com/news/post-nation/wp/2014/11/26/officials-release-video-names-in-fatal-police-shooting-of-12-year-old-cleveland-boy/; Joseph Goldstein & Nate Schweber, Man's Death After Chokehold Raises Old Issue for the Police, N.Y. TIMES (July 18, 2014), available at http://www.nytimes.com/2014/07/19/nyregion/staten-island-man-dies-after-he-is-put-in-chokehold-during-arrest.html? _r=1; Richard Pérez-Peña, University of Cincinnati Officer Indicted in Shooting Death of Samuel Debose, N.Y TIMES (July 29, 2015), available at http://www.nytimes.com/2015/07/30/us/university-of-cincinnati-officer-indicted-inshooting-death-of-motorist.html; Scott Malone & Ian Simpson, Six Baltimore

Officers Charged in the Death of Freddie Gray, One With Murder, REUTERS (May 1, 2015), available at http://www.reuters.com/article/2015/05/01/us-usapolice-baltimore-idUSKBN0NL1GO20150501; Mark Berman, South Carolina Police Officer in Walter Scott Shooting Indicted on Murder Charge, WASH. POST (June 8, 2015), available at http://www.washingtonpost.com/news/postnation/wp/2015/06/08/police-officer-who-shot-walter-scott-indicted-for-murder/.

[6] FINAL REPORT, THE PRESIDENT'S TASK FORCE ON 21ST CENTURY POLICING (2015), available at http://www.cops.usdoj.gov/pdf/taskforce/taskforce_finalreport.pdf.

[7] Policing Strategies for the 21st Century, Hearing Before the H. Comm. on the Judiciary, 114th Cong. (2015), available at http://judiciary.house.gov/index.cfm/hearings?ID=9F5ABE57-E0F0-468E-9B79-F9DFDC448E11.

[8] See Campaign Zero, Limit Use of Force (last visited Sept. 28, 2015), http://www.joincampaignzero.org/force.

[9] See, e.g., id. (statement of Sheriff David Clarke, Jr., Milwaukee County, Wisconsin); D.C. McAllister, Activists Use Charges of Police Racism to Justify a Huge Power Grab, THE FEDERALIST (June 12, 2015), available at http://thefederalist.com/2015/06/12/activists-use-charges-of-police-racism-to-justify-a-huge-power-grab/.

[10] Civil Rights Act of 1871, ch. 22, § 1, 17 Stat. 13, (codified at 42 U.S.C. § 1983).

[11] Civil Rights Act of 1866, 18 U.S.C. § 242.

[12] 42 U.S.C. § 14141.

[13] Note that an assessment of the legality of specific instances of force, such as in Ferguson or elsewhere, or an evaluation of use of force rules under state law, are beyond the scope of this report.

[14] Depending on the setting of the police-citizen encounter, different constitutional provisions might apply. For seizures occurring during an "arrest, investigatory stop, or other 'seizure' of a free citizen," the Fourth Amendment applies. See U.S. CONST. amend. IV; Graham v. Connor, 490 U.S. 386, 395 (1989). If the alleged excessive force was used after the person was arrested and while they were in detention, the Due Process Clause's "shock the conscience" standard will apply. U.S CONST. amends. V & XIV. Force used against a person that has already been convicted and is incarcerated is subject to the prohibition on "cruel and unusual" punishment as protected under the Eighth Amendment. U.S. CONST. amend. VIII.

[15] U.S. CONST. amend. IV.

[16] See Johnson v. Glik, 481 F.2d 1028, 1033 (2d Cir. 1973) (applying substantive due process standard to claims of excessive force); Franklin v. Aycock, 795 F.2d 1253, 1258 (6th Cir. 1986) (same); Burton v. Livingston, 791 F.2d 97, 100 (8th Cir. 1986) (same). But see Lester v. City of Chicago, 830 F.2d 706, 711 (7th Cir. 1987) (applying Fourth Amendment to claims of excessive force).

Judge Henry Friendly's prominent use of force test in Glik assessed (1) "the need for the application of force," (2) "the relationship between the need and the amount of force that was used," (3) "the extent of injury inflicted," and (4) "whether force was applied in a good faith effort to maintain or restore discipline or maliciously and sadistically for the very purpose of causing harm." Johnson, 481 F.2d at 1033.

[17] Judge Friendly's four-part test from Glik remains the appropriate standard when assessing force used during post-arrest, pre-trial detention. See, e.g., United States v. Cobb, 905 F.3d 784, 788 (4th Cir. 1990) (instructing jury in 18 U.S.C. § 242 case using Glik standard).

[18] Tennessee v. Garner, 471 U.S. 1 (1985).

[19] Id. at 5.

[20] TENN. CODE ANN. § 40-7-108 (1982).
[21] Garner, 471 U.S. at 7 (quoting United States v. Brignoni-Ponce, 422 U.S. 873, 878 (1975)).
[22] Garner, 471 U.S. at 7 (quoting United States v. Place, 462 U.S. 696, 703 (1983)).
[23] Id. at 9.
[24] Id. at 11.
[25] Id. at 11-12.
[26] Graham v. Connor, 490 U.S. 386 (1989).
[27] Id. at 389.
[28] Id. at 395 (emphasis in original).
[29] Id. at 396.
[30] Id.
[31] Id. at 396.
[32] Id. at 396-97.
[33] Id. at 397.
[34] Id.
[35] See Whren v. United States, 517 U.S. 806, 813 (1996) (rejecting argument that "constitutional reasonableness of traffic stop depends on the actual motivations of individual officers involved").
[36] Scott v. Harris, 550 U.S. 372 (2007).
[37] Id. at 375.
[38] Id.
[39] Id. at 383.
[40] Id. at 386.
[41] See Karen M. Blum, Scott v. Harris: Death Knell for Deadly Force Policies and Garner Jury Instructions?, 58 SYRACUSE L. REV. 45, 54 (2007).
[42] Id. at 59-60.
[43] See Blake v. City of New York, No. 05-6652, 2007 WL 1975570, *3-4 (S.D.N.Y. July 6, 2007) (internal citations omitted).
[44] Rahn v. Hawkins, 464 F.3d 813, 818 (8th Cir. 2006).
[45] Montoute v. Carr, 114 F.3d 181, 185 (11th Cir. 1997).
[46] Ayala v. Wolfe, 546 Fed. Appx.197, 202 (4th Cir. 2013).
[47] See, e.g., Thompson v. Hubbard, 257 F.3d 896, 899 (8th Cir. 2001) ("An officer is not constitutionally required to wait until he sets eyes upon the weapon before employing deadly force to protect himself against a fleeing suspect who turns and moves as though to draw a gun."); Lamont v. New Jersey, 637 F.3d 177 (3d Cir. 2011) (holding that officer's mistaken belief that suspect was drawing a weapon that turned out to be a crack pipe did not render use of deadly force unreasonable); Dudley v. Eden, 260 F.3d 722, 727 (6th Cir. 2001).
[48] See Harrell v. Decatur County, 22 F.3d 1570, 1578 (11th Cir. 1994) (Dubina, dissenting), majority opinion vacated Harrell v. Decatur County, 41 F.3d 1494, 1494 (11th Cir. 1995).
[49] See Anderson v. Russell, 247 F.3d 125, 130-31 (4th Cir. 2001).
[50] Edwards v. City of Martins Ferry, 554 F. Supp. 2d 797, 804 (S.D. Ohio 2008).
[51] See Plakas v. Drinksi, 19 F.3d 1143, 1149 (7th Cir. 1994); Scott v. Heinrich, 39 F.3d 912, 915 (9th Cir. 1994); Jiron v. City of Lakewood, 392 F.3d 410, 414 (10th Cir. 2004); see generally Illinois v. Lafayette, 462 U.S. 640, 647 (1983) ("The reasonableness of any particular governmental activity does not necessarily or invariably turn on the existence of alternative 'less intrusive' means.").
[52] Heinrich, 39 F.3d at 915.

[53] Lowe v. City of Seattle, No. 07-0784, 2008 WL 4083150 *6 (W.D. Wash. Aug. 29, 2008).

[54] Cooper v. Sheehan, 735 F.3d 153 (4th Cir. 2013).

[55] Id.

[56] Id.

[57] Scott v. Harris, 550 U.S. 372, 386 (2007).

[58] Mattos v. Agaronos, 661 F.3d 433, 441 (9th Cir. 2011) (internal quotation marks omitted); see also George v. Morris, 736 F.3d 829, 838 (9th Cir. 2013).

[59] See Penney v. Eslinger, 605 F.3d 843, 850 (11th Cir. 2010); see also Beshers v. Harrison, 495 F.3d 1260, 1267 (11th Cir. 2007) (Recently ... in Scott v. Harris, the Supreme Court limited Garner's applicability.).

[60] Rasanen v. Doe, 723 F.3d 325, 334 (2d Cir. 2013).

[61] Cooper v. Sheehan, 735 F.3d 153, 159 (4th Cir. 2013) (citing to Garner and noting that "[a] reasonable officer is entitled to use deadly force '[w]here the officer has probable cause to believe that [a] suspect poses a threat of serious physical harm, either to the officer or to others.'").

[62] See Sanchez v. Fraley, 376 Fed. Appx. 449, 451 (5th Cir. 2010) (citing to Garner and noting that "when an officer uses deadly force, our 'objective reasonableness' balancing test is constrained.").

[63] See Krause v. Jones, 765 F.3d 675, 680 (6th Cir. 2014).

[64] Rasanen v. Brown, 841 F. Supp. 2d 687, 697-98 (E.D.N.Y. 2012), vac'd sub nom., 723 F.3d 325 (2d Cir. 2013).

[65] Rasanen, 723 F.3d at 334.

[66] Id. at 333.

[67] J. David Goodman & Al Baker, Wave of Protests After Grand Jury Doesn't Indict Officer in Eric Garner Chokehold Case, N.Y. TIMES (Dec. 3, 2014), available at http://www.nytimes.com/2014/12/04/nyregion/grand-jury-said-to-bringno-charges-in-staten-island-chokehold-death-of-eric-garner.html?_r=0.

[68] Editorial Board, Questions Still Remain Over the Death of Natasha McKenna, WASH. POST (Sept. 8, 2015), available at https://www.washingtonpost.com/opinions/an-accounting-but-not-the-end/2015/09/08/5660cc4c-5670-11e5-abe9- 27d53f250b11_story.html; Wesley Lowery, Two Former Ga. Police Officers Charged with Murder for Stun Gun Death of Handcuffed Man, WASH. POST (Aug. 18 2015), available at https://www.washingtonpost.com/news/post-nation/wp/ 2015/08/18/two-former-ga-police-officers-charged-with-murder-for-stun-gun-death-of-handcuffed-man/.

[69] Associated Press, Authorities: Man Dies After Being Pepper Sprayed By Police, N.Y. TIMES (July 11, 2015), available at http://www.nytimes.com/aponline/2015/07/11/us/ap-us-pepper-spray-police-death.html.

[70] See U.S. Dep't of Justice, Office of Community Oriented Policing Services, After-Action Assessment of the Police Response to the August 2014 Demonstrations in Ferguson, Missouri (2015); Ferguson Protestors File Lawsuit Against Police for "Excessive Use of Force", The Guardian (Aug. 29, 2014), available at http://www.theguardian.com/world/2014/aug/29/ferguson-protesters-lawsuit-police-excessive-force.

[71] AMNESTY INTERNATIONAL, AMNESTY INTERNATIONAL'S CONCERNS ABOUT DEATHS AND ILL-TREATMENT INVOLVING POLICE USE OF TASERS 1 (2004) [hereinafter Amnesty International 2004 Report].

"Taser" is the name for a particular type of conducted energy device (the technical name for these less-lethal weapons), but it is commonly used to refer to all types of conducted energy devices, much like photocopiers are commonly called "Xerox" machines.

[72] U.S Dep't of Justice, Bureau of Justice Statistics, Local Police Departments, 2013: Equipment and Technology (2013), available at http://www.bjs.gov/content/pub/pdf/lpd13et.pdf.

[73] Amnesty International, USA: Stricter Limits Urged as Deaths Following Police Taser Use Reach 500 (Feb. 15, 2012), available at https://www.amnesty.org/en/latest/news/2012/02/usa-stricter-limits-urged-deaths-following-policetaser-use-reach/.

[74] Amnesty International 2004 Report, supra note 71, at 4; see also Taser International, Inc., Taser Electronic Control Devices Electrical Characteristics (Feb. 1, 2009), available at http://www.ecdlaw.info/outlines/EC_02-01- 09_%20X26_Elec_Char.pdf.

[75] Amnesty International 2004 Report, supra note 71, at 5.

[76] Brown v. City of Golden Valley, 574 F.3d 491, 499 (8th Cir. 2009).

[77] Id. at 500.

[78] Id. at 494.

[79] Id. at 498.

[80] See Roberts v. Manigold, 240 Fed. Appx. 675, 678 (6th Cir. 2007).

[81] See Zivojinovich v. Barner, 525 F.3d 1270, 1278 (11th Cir. 2008).

[82] Johnson v. City of Lincoln Park, 434 F. Supp. 2d 467, 480 (E.D. Mich. 2006).

[83] Buckley v. Haddock, 292 Fed. Appx. 791, 792-93 (11th Cir. 2008).

[84] Id. at 794.

[85] Id. at 807.

[86] Id.

[87] See Lowe v. City of Seattle, No. 07-0784, 2008 WL 4083150 (W.D. Wash. Aug. 29, 2008).

[88] Id. at *6.

[89] See, e.g., Draper v. Reynolds, 369 F.3d 1270, 1278 (11th Cir. 2004); Lowe, 2008 WL 4083150, at *6 ("[P]laintiff was not seriously injured, and she received treatment both at the scene and at Harborview immediately after.").

[90] Draper, 369 F.3d at 1278.

[91] Michaels v. City of Vermillion, 539 F. Supp. 2d 975, 987 (N.D. Ohio 2008).

[92] See Moretta v. Abbott, 280 Fed. Appx. 823, 825 (11th Cir. 2008).

[93] See Casey v. City of Federal Heights, 509 F.3d 1278, 1282-83 (10th Cir. 2007); Buckley v. Haddock, 292 Fed. Appx. 791, 795 (11th Cir. 2008).

[94] See Phillip Kennicott, US Davis Pepper Spraying Raises Questions About Role of Police, WASH. POST. (Nov. 20, 2011), available at https://www.washingtonpost.com/lifestyle/style/uc-davis-pepper-spraying-raises-questions-aboutrole-of-police/2011/11/20/gIQAOr8dfN_story.html; Maura Judkis, Occupy's 84-year-old Pepper Spray Victim: Is this the Most Iconic Image of the Movement?, Wash. Post (Nov. 16, 2011), available at http://www.washingtonpost.com/ blogs/arts-post/post/occupys-84-year-old-pepper-spray-victim-is-this-the-most-iconic-image-of-the-movement/2011/11/16/gIQAzateRN_blog.html.

[95] See German Lopez, Cops in Ferguson Hit A Photojournalist with Pepper Spray. Then Something Amazing Happened, VOX (Aug. 11, 2015), available at http://www.vox.com/2015/8/11/9130221/ferguson-pepper-spray.

[96] NAT'L INST. OF JUSTICE, OLEORESIN CAPSICUM: PEPPER SPRAY AS A FORCE ALTERNATIVE 1 (1994).

[97] Park v. Shiflett, 250 F.3d 843, 849 (4th Cir. 2001).

[98] See, e.g., Young v. County of Los Angeles, 655 F.3d 1156, 1159 (9th Cir. 2011); Headwaters Forest Defense v. County of Humboldt, 240 F.3d 1185, 1205-06 (2000); Adams v. Metiva, 31 F.3d 375, 386 (6th Cir. 1994); Greene v. Barber, 310 F.3d 889, 898 (6th Cir. 2002).

[99] See Young, 655 F.3d at 1167.

[100] See Headwaters Forest Defense v. County of Humboldt, 240 F.3d 1185, 1205-06 (2000). The Supreme Court granted certiorari in this case, vacated the decision, and remanded the case for further consideration in light of Saucier v. Katz, 533 U.S. 194 (2001), which altered the way qualified immunity cases are evaluated. Upon reevaluating the case, the Ninth Circuit's original ruling on the Fourth Amendment merits of the officer's use of force was not altered. See Headwaters Forest Defense Fund v. County of Humboldt, 276 F.3d 1125 (9th Cir. 2002).

[101] Id. at 1205.

[102] Singleton v. Darby, 609 Fed. Appx. 190, 195 (5th Cir. 2015).

[103] Id.

[104] See, e.g., Vinyard v. Wilson, 311 F.3d 1340, 1347-348 (11th Cir. 2002); Park v. Shiflett, 250 F.3d 843, 853 (4th Cir. 2001).

[105] See U.S. CONST. amend. XIV; Lugar v. Edmonton Oil Co., Inc., 457 U.S. 922 (1982) (quoting Lynch v. Household Finance Corp., 405 U.S. 538, 545 (1972) (Section 1983 was enacted "for the express purpose of 'enforc [ing] the Provisions of the Fourteenth Amendment.'"); see also CRS Report R44104, Federal Power over Local Law Enforcement Reform: Legal Issues, by Jared P. Cole.

[106] See United States v. Classic, 313 U.S. 299, 326-27 (1941).

[107] 18 U.S.C. § 242.

[108] See Classic, 313 U.S. at 326-27.

[109] See Rachel Harmon, Promoting Civil Rights Through Proactive Police Reform, 62 STAN. L. REV. 1, 9 (2009) ("Federal criminal civil rights prosecutions face significant legal and practical obstacles, including that federal law imposes an onerous intent requirement on civil rights crimes; that victims of police misconduct often make problematic witnesses; and that juries frequently believe and sympathize with defendant officers"); Stephen Rushin, Federal Enforcement of Police Reform, 82 FORDHAM L. REV. 3189, 3203 (2014) (noting DOJ's lack of resources to bring civil rights criminal prosecutions).

[110] Rushin, supra note 109.

[111] See Michael J. Pastor, A Tragedy and a Crime? Amadou Diallo, Specific Intent, and the Federal Prosecution of Civil Rights Violations, 6 N.Y.U. J. LEGIS. & PUB. POL'Y 171 (2002-2003).

[112] Act of April 1866, ch. 31, § 2.

[113] Act of March 4, 1909, 35 Stat. 1092.

[114] 43 Cong. Rec. 60th Cong., 2d Sess., p. 3599.

[115] TRAC REPORTS, UNDER COLOR OF LAW (2004), available at http://trac.syr.edu/tracreports/civright/107/.

[116] Screws v. United States, 325 U.S. 91, 92 (1945).

[117] Id.

[118] Id.

[119] Id. at 93.

[120] Id. at 95.

[121] Id.

[122] Id. at 96.

[123] Id.

[124] Id. at 97.

[125] Id. at 101.

[126] Id.

[127] Id. at 106.

[128] See United States v. Johnstone, 107 F.3d 200, 208 (3d Cir. 1997).

[129] One way to reconcile these statements is to say that the officer need not be thinking "I want to invade this suspect's Fourth Amendment right to be free from unreasonable seizures," but rather need only be thinking, "I am going to apply more force than I think is reasonable in these circumstances." In this situation, the officer is not necessarily thinking in constitutional terms, but is intentionally applying more force than he thinks is reasonable, beyond that which he was instructed during his training.

[130] Screws, 325 U.S. at 104.

[131] Id.

[132] Johnstone, 107 F.3d at 208.

[133] United States v. Garza, 754 F.2d 1202, 1204 (5th Cir. 1985).

[134] Id. at 1209.

[135] Id.

[136] United States v. Kerley, 643 F.2d 299, 303 (5th Cir. 1981).

[137] Id. at 301.

[138] Id. at 303.

[139] Id.

[140] United States v. Shafer, 384 F. Supp. 496, 503 (N.D. Ohio 1974).

[141] United States v. Cobb, 905 F.2d 784, 785 (4th Cir. 1990).

[142] Id. at 788.

[143] Id. at 789.

[144] United States v. Johnstone, 107 F.3d 200, 208 (3d Cir. 1997).

[145] Id. at 208 n.11.

[146] Id.

[147] Id.

[148] As the Third Circuit notes, the Supreme Court suggested in dicta in Farmers v. Brennan that the subjective approach was the appropriate test to apply in § 242 cases. See id. (citing Farmers v. Brennan, 511 U.S. 825, 839 n.7 (1994)).

[149] United States v. Gwaltney, 790 F.2d 1378, 1386 (9th Cir. 1986).

[150] Mark Joseph Stern, Why the Feds Can't Charge Darren Wilson, SLATE (Nov. 26, 2014), available at http://www.slate.com/articles/news_and_politics/jurisprudence/2014/11/ will_ justice_department_charge_darren_wilson_supreme_court_gutted_civil.html.

[151] U.S. Comm. on Civil Rights, Revisiting Who is Guarding the Guardians: A Report on Police Practices and Civil Rights in America (2000), available at http://www.usccr.gov/ pubs/guard/ch5.htm#_ftnref7.

[152] In re Winship, 397 U.S. 358, 364 (1970).

[153] Civil Rights Act of 1871, ch. 22, § 1, 17 Stat. 13.

[154] 42 U.S.C. § 1983. Section 1983 is directed solely at state and local actors and does not apply to federal law enforcement officers. However, the Supreme Court interpreted the Fourth Amendment to include an implied cause of action against federal officers in Bivens v. Six Unknown Named Agents of Fed. Bureau of Narcotics, 403 U.S. 388, 397 (1971).

[155] Graham v. Connor, 490 U.S. 386, 393-94 (1989) (quoting Baker v. McCollan, 443 U.S. 137, 144 n.3 (1979) (internal quotation marks omitted)).

[156] West v. Atkins, 487 U.S. 42, 48 (1988).

[157] Daniels v. Williams, 474 U.S. 327, 329-30 (1986).

[158] MARTIN A. SCHWARTZ, SECTION 1983 LITIG. CLAIMS & DEFENSES § 16.01 (2015).

[159] Harlow v. Fitzgerald, 457 U.S. 800, 818 (1982).

[160] Pearson v. Callahan, 555 U.S. 223, 231 (2009).

[161] Malley v. Briggs, 475 U.S. 335, 341 (1986).

[162] See Diana Hassel, Excessive Reasonableness, 43 INDIANA L. REV. 117, 118 (2009) ("The Court's development of the qualified immunity doctrine has stretched the rationale underlying the defense to a breaking point. Instead of providing protection only to those government actors who violate the law unwittingly and reasonably, qualified immunity has metastasized into an almost absolute defense to all but the most outrageous conduct.").

[163] Saucier v. Katz, 533 U.S. 194, 201 (2001).

[164] Purtell v. Mason, 527 F.3d 615, 622 (7th Cir. 2008).

[165] Pearson, 555 U.S. at 236.

[166] Id.

[167] Anderson v. Creighton, 483 U.S. 635, 640 (1987). The qualified immunity test is the same under both § 1983 and Bivens. See Wilson v. Layne, 526 U.S. 603, 609 (1999).

[168] Hope v. Pelzer, 536 U.S. 730, 741 (2002).

[169] Anderson, 483 U.S. at 639.

[170] Ashcroft v. al-Kidd, 563 U.S. 731, ___, 131 S. Ct. 2074, 2084 (2011).

[171] Id. at 2083.

[172] Tennessee v. Garner, 471 U.S. 1 (1985).

[173] Graham v. Connor, 490 U.S. 386 (1989).

[174] Scott v. Harris, 550 U.S. 372 (2007).

[175] Scott, 550 U.S. at 383.

[176] Wilson v. City of Lafayette, 510 F. App'x 775, 777 (10th Cir.).

[177] See, e.g., 745 ILL. COMP. STAT. § 10/9-102; MO. ANN. STAT. § 105.711; Joanna Schwartz, Police Indemnification, 89 N.Y.U. L REV. 885, 885 (2014) ("Through public records requests, interviews, and other sources, I have collected information about indemnification practices in forty-four of the largest law enforcement agencies across the country, and in thirty-seven small and mid-sized agencies. My study reveals that police officers are virtually always indemnified: During the study period, governments paid approximately 99.98% of the dollars that plaintiffs recovered in lawsuits alleging civil rights violations by law enforcement.").

[178] Hudson v. Michigan, 547 U.S. 586, 597 (2006).

[179] Monell v. Department of Social Services of New York, 436 U.S. 658 (1978).

[180] Id. at 694.

[181] Id.

[182] Id. at 388.

[183] Id. at 390.

[184] Bd. of Cnty. Comm'rs of Bryan Cnty., Okl. v. Brown, 520 U.S. 397, 405 (1997).

[185] Id. at 405.

[186] Id. at 415-16.

[187] See Los Angeles v. Lyons, 461 U.S. 95, 97-98 (1983); United States v. City of Philadelphia, 644 F.2d 187, 206 (3d Cir. 1980).

[188] 42 U.S.C. §14141.

[189] See generally Police Executive Research Forum, Civil Rights Investigations of Local Police: Lessons Learned, (2013), http://www.policeforum.org/assets/docs/Critical_Issues_Series/civil%20rights%20investigations%20of%20local%20police%20-%20lessons%20learned%202013.pdf.

[190] United States v. City of New Orleans, No. 12-1924 (E.D. La. July 24, 2012) (consent decree regarding the New Orleans Police Department), available at http://www.nola.gov/

getattachment/NOPD/About-Us/NOPD-ConsentDecree/NOPD-Consent-Decree-7-24-12.pdf/.

[191] See Samuel Walker, The New Paradigm of Police Accountability: The U.S. Justice Department "Pattern or Practice" Suits In Context, 22 ST. LOUIS U PUB. L. REV. 6 (2003).

[192] H.R. 2052, 114th Cong. (2015).

[193] See 18 U.S.C. § 242.

[194] H.R. 1102, 114th Cong. (2015).

[195] See CRS Report R44104, Federal Power over Local Law Enforcement Reform: Legal Issues, by Jared P. Cole.

[196] H.R. 306, 114th Cong. (2015).

[197] See CRS Report RS22416, Edward Byrne Memorial Justice Assistance Grant (JAG) Program, by Nathan James, for an overview of the JAG program.

[198] Exec. Order No. 13684, Establishment of the President's Task Force on 21st Century Policing, 79 Fed. Reg. 76865 (Dec. 23, 2014).

[199] Final Report, President's Task Force, supra note 6, at 20-22.

[200] Pastor, supra note 111.

[201] John V. Jacobi, Prosecuting Police Misconduct, 2000 WISC. L. REV. 789 (2000).

[202] Guarding the Guardians, supra note 151 ("The burdensome standards imposed by the courts severely limiting the liability of municipalities for the unlawful conduct of their police officers often leave victims with no real remedy.").

[203] Myriam E. Giles, Reinventing Structural Reform Litigation: Deputizing Private Citizens in the Enforcement of Civil Rights, 100 COLUM. L. REV. 1384, 1386 (2000).

In: Police Use of Force …
Editor: Beverly Guzman
ISBN: 978-1-63484-557-1

Chapter 2

STATEMENT OF MATTHEW BARGE, VICE PRESIDENT & DEPUTY DIRECTOR, POLICE ASSESSMENT RESOURCE CENTER. HEARING ON "POLICING STRATEGIES FOR THE 21ST CENTURY"*

Chairman Goodlatte, Ranking Member Conyers, and distinguished members of the Committee:

My name is Matthew Barge. I am the Vice President and Deputy Director of the Police Assessment Resource Center (PARC). I appreciate the opportunity to appear before you and provide an independent perspective on the substantial challenges and opportunities that our local police departments face.

In light of recent high-profile incidents involving local law enforcement agencies and related unrest in several communities across the country, attention has appropriately turned to figuring out what police strategies and approaches best promote effective, safe, and constitutional policing. However, these efforts to identify best practices go back decades.

Some have wondered whether police agencies in our local communities are capable of changing or of proactively reforming themselves. My organization, PARC, has a long history of providing independent, evidence-based counsel on effective, respectful, and publicly accountable policing. A

---

* This is an edited, reformatted and augmented version of a statement presented May 19, 2015 before the House Judiciary Committee.

nonprofit organization with offices in New York and Los Angeles, it was founded in 2001 by the Vera Institute of Justice, and with the generous support of the Ford Foundation. PARC is not an advocacy organization. Instead, it is committed to serving as an honest broker that helps law enforcement agencies solve problems by incorporating best practices, managing risks, using data-driven management, and providing services with greater efficiency and accountability. We do all of this with an eye toward increasing officer safety, public safety, and public confidence in the police. PARC has assisted upward of 30 agencies, local governments, or community organizations in these efforts in its 14 years in existence.

In our experience, police departments can change and they are changing. Local governments and police agencies themselves regularly call on PARC to conduct comprehensive assessments of where their departments are, where they should be, and what they need to do in order to align with best practices with respect to accountability and effectiveness. In Portland, Oregon, for example, PARC conducted a review of officer-involved shootings and made recommendations for changes in policy, training, and practice. The implementation of those recommendations led to an 88% drop in officer-involved shootings, a 59% decrease in use of force, and a 51% decrease in citizen s complaints all without increases in officer injuries or crime.[1] Likewise, for some 21 years, Los Angeles County engaged PARC s Executive Director to serve as special counsel for monitoring the Los Angeles County Sheriffs Department, the fourth-largest law enforcement agency in the U.S. The effort produced results with respect to officer training, citizen s complaints, medical care in jails, recruitment and hiring, anti-gang strategies, and many other areas.[2]

In some instances, however, more sustained attention at the national level is necessary. One consequence of our democracy is that police authority is highly fragmented. The most recent data indicate that we have more than 12,000 local police departments that employ roughly 477,000 full-time police officers. Nearly half of these departments employ no more than 10 officers.[3] Some departments fail to identify problems in their relationship with the community, deficiencies in officer oversight, or problems in how its officers use force or detain subjects. Many departments either do not have access to enough useful information about [law] suits involving their officers or intentionally ignore information from suits relating to problematic incidents.[4] Patterns or practices of unlawful policing can take hold.

When problems fester in local police departments, the U.S. Department of Justice (DOJ) may exercise the authority granted by this body[5] to conduct an investigation into alleged patterns of misconduct within a police department with respect to excessive force, discriminatory policing, unlawful stops and searches, and other constitutional violations. Where the allegations are substantiated, those investigations can lead to agreements between the Department of Justice and the involved local jurisdiction, with input from community stakeholders, to implement a package of reforms and remedial measures.

Some of the DOJ settlements take the form of federal-court-overseen consent decrees. The consent decree process is akin to emergency open-heart surgery for police departments. It addresses serious, systemic issues that have built up over time. It is a major intervention that, historically, the Department of Justice has used selectively, at critical moments, and where rigorous and sustained intervention is needed. It is intended to last no longer, but end no sooner, than it takes for the identified problems to be effectively remedied while ensuring officer and public safety. In the past three years, DOJ successfully concluded implementation of two major consent decrees addressing the Los Angeles Police Department and District of Columbia Metropolitan Police Department.

Currently, the Department of Justice is enforcing ten federal-court-overseen consent decrees. PARC s Executive Director, Merrick Bobb, serves as the federal court-appointed, independent monitor of one of those decrees, which relates to the Seattle Police Department (SPD). I serve as his deputy, overseeing a nationwide network of law enforcement experts. Mr. Bobb has nearly 25 years of experience with law enforcement issues, starting with the blue-ribbon commission chaired by Warren Christopher to reform the Los Angeles Police Department (LAPD) in the wake of the Rodney King incident in the early 1990s.

Whether reform is self-initiated, occurs to conform with national standards like those of the Commission on Accreditation for Law Enforcement Agencies (CALEA), or occurs pursuant to a federal investigation or DOJ settlement, the bedrock of policing in the 21st century must be a strong, responsive relationship between the nation s police departments and the communities that they serve.

To that end, a common playbook of specific, real-world practices and reforms is emerging for ensuring the safety of the public and officers, advance efficient law enforcement, protect constitutional rights, and enhance public trust in the police across America s diverse communities. The challenges are substantial, and the work is hard but law enforcement agencies can today make reforms that we know work in order to enhance accountability and trust. The remainder of my testimony will summarize these areas.

I. USE OF FORCE

A. Policy & Training

Officers need clearer, more specific, and more pragmatic guidelines on when they may use force in the field and what level of force is permissive in a given case. This is especially true when Court decisions directly situate the constitutionality of force in terms of the facts and circumstances confronting an officer in a given situation[6] and expressly disclaim the existence a magical on/off switch that triggers rigid preconditions that make some force appropriate and some inappropriate.[7] Although general standards and balancing tests may be fair and workable for courts, officers in the real world and the communities that they serve need and deserve clear expectations and pragmatic rules for when force is justified.

Any use of force policy must balance concision with precision and broad applicability. It must guide officers across innumerable unforeseen circumstances yet be specific enough to permit a department to hold officers accountable for using inferior tactics or poor decision-making.

For example, the DOJ-, Monitor-, and Court-approved officer use of force policy in Seattle requires that all officer force be necessary, reasonable, proportional to the danger or threat posed by the subject, and used when no reasonable alternatives to de-escalate were available However, absent limited exceptional circumstances, it prohibits officers from using force on restrained or handcuffed subjects. That provision directly responds to the Department of Justice s finding in its 2011 investigation that SPD had previously engage[d] in a pattern or practice of using excessive force against individuals who are already under control and who, consequently, under most circumstances does not pose an immediate threat to the safety of the officer or the public. 8

Thus, SPD policy provides greater clarity on how to use force in particular circumstances based on the history of that particular Department and concerns of the community that it serves. PARC has similarly assisted a number of other agencies in crafting specific use of force policies tailored to the concerns and histories of their own communities.

Every police department in the United States has the same opportunity to set forth clear and specific policies on when force may be used that reflect the values of the community and organization and go further than the bare, often vague requirements of the courts in the area and to doggedly insist on strict adherence to the policies as preconditions for continued employment with the department.

As the recent national dialogue has proceeded, a consensus has started to emerge that departments should emphasize the importance of de-escalation or slowing down and defusing situations in a manner that might lessen or eliminate the possibility that an officer will need to contemplate force at all.[9] These tactics include strategic use of distance, cover, and concealment; verbal techniques aimed toward persuasion or the promotion or rational decision-making; and calling for more or more specialized officers to the scene. The goal is to maximize opportunities for incidents and interactions to conclude without officers needing to use force.

Seattle, under the Department of Justice consent decree, is also leading the way in de-escalation. There, officers are *required* by policy to use de-escalation tactics whenever safe under the circumstances and time and circumstances permit.[10] No longer are these tactics taught as an extra skill or course disconnected from the real tactical concerns of firearms or Taser training. Instead, they are being woven throughout more than 32 hours of training this year alone, with de-escalation presented as often the best strategic option and valuable both to officers and the communities that they serve.

Because it increases officer safety and mitigates the need to use force, de-escalation training is being adopted by law enforcement agencies nationwide. Training on defusing critical incidents has been recently embraced by the New York Police Department[11], Pennsylvania[12], and several other agencies. Departments in Oakland and Dallas are providing stress inoculation training geared toward providing officers with superior decision-making skills in high-stress incidents.

B. Officer Training on Mental Health & Behavioral Issues

At least half of officer-involved shootings involve a subject experiencing mental health issues and the numbers are higher than that in some communities.[13] Meanwhile, officers increasingly feel as though the burdens of failures elsewhere in our social service networks fall ever more to them.

Departments from Las Vegas to Dallas, and Chicago to the United States Capitol Police Department, are responding by providing specialized training on identifying and interacting with subjects with behavioral and mental health issues.[14] These crisis intervention programs have produced real results. For instance, after providing expanded crisis training to officers and establishing a dedicated team to address individuals experiencing a behavioral crisis, the Oakland Police Department reduced its overall use of force by some 50 percent. Use of force and officer injuries both declined sharply in the years following implementation of a crisis intervention program in Memphis. In Seattle, the Consent Decree has resulted in a regional committee of health experts, clinicians, community advocates, academics, members of the judiciary, and the police to situate the Police Department s efforts to respond to individuals experiencing behavioral crisis.

A number of national organizations, including the International Association of Chiefs of Police (IACP) and the National Alliance on Mental Illness (NAMI), [15] have endorsed the implementation of crisis intervention programs. Crisis intervention is an important part of most DOJ settlements in the policing area, and the number of good off-the-shelf training programs makes this a reform that is effective, is affordable, and increases officer and public safety.

II. Administrative Inefficiency & Internal Accountability

Many police agencies resemble what might happen if the stereotypical Department of Motor Vehicles ran the U.S. military: an inefficient, inept bureaucracy overseeing a necessarily rigid command-and-control structure empowered to use force. This produces a law enforcement culture often resistant to new approaches and systems. Officers tend to be rewarded and promoted for staying in their lanes, not making difficult decisions or challenging the *status quo*. Pushing paper substitutes for real accountability and meaningful oversight of what officers are actually doing on the streets. In some jurisdictions, well-intentioned police chiefs have difficulty replacing problem employees because of civil service protections or state employment laws.

Accordingly, a major focus of any reform effort, whether initiated by the local community or the federal government, must be on basic organizational reform making ossified bureaucracies and ineffective administrative processes more nimble, responsive, innovative, and transparent. In a number of important areas, police departments simply need to become more comfortable with change and new ways of doing business. The day-to-day operational culture of many agencies must change.

For example, just as doctors present cases to peers and even winning teams review game footage, law enforcement agencies must commit to processes and procedures for comprehensively analyzing the performance of officers and holding them accountable. Some of the best departments have a dedicated Force Review Board that reviews, analyzes, and evaluates all uses of force so that the department can perpetually update its training, tactics, procedure, and policy in light of lessons learned about how officers are operating in the real world. It is a standard part of the Department of Justice s settlements in the police area and constitutes a best practice. The challenge is to make members of these, and other similar, mechanisms for critical self-analysis comfortable with the notion of evaluating the conduct of another officer. As uncomfortable as this exercise may be at first, it is necessary to enable departments to learn from the past and better prepare their officers to face problems in the field more safely and appropriately.

Citizens have a role in eliminating administrative inefficiency and promoting accountability, as well. Permanent civilian oversight mechanisms whether taking the form of a civilian board that investigates or reviews complaints about the police, an institutional inspector general or monitor to conduct larger-scale assessments of departmental trends, or an auditor who reviews completed internal investigations[16] can give communities a real-time check on police authority and a say in how policing is conducted.

Several jurisdictions, including Eugene, Oregon and Milwaukee, Wisconsin, have affirmatively sought PARC s counsel in helping it decide what form or structure of civilian oversight might best address their concerns. Likewise, the DOJ consent decree process often inspires this greater and more formal involvement in the nuts and bolts of police oversight and accountability. Just a few weeks ago, Newark, New Jersey created one of the country s strongest civilian police-review boards that will have subpoena power and make binding recommendations as it enters into a consent decree.[17] The Seattle decree created a Community Police Commission to provide input and policy recommendations during the reform process.

Too often, community policing means talking at communities or organizing isolated, small-scale initiatives. For trust to be restored between the community and police where it has frayed, the community needs to be an ongoing part of policing in significant, structural ways.

III. DATA-DRIVEN POLICING

As memorialized in the book and movie *Moneyball*, the 2002 Oakland Athletics and then-general manager Billy Beane famously used sophisticated data analytics and an evidence-based management approach to improve performance on the baseball field. Many departments are, however, a long way from playing Moneyball.

Currently, too many police agencies have no idea how often their officers use force, are involved in shootings, or make stops. If data exists, it is often inaccurate, inaccessible, or ignored. In one police department where PARC has recently worked, a supervisor wanting to know whether or when an officer had been trained to use the Taser an important, less-lethal force instrument would have to manually sift through stacks of unorganized 3 x 5 index cards. One of the reasons that there is no reliable national data on how many people are shot by police officers each year [18] is because many police departments themselves are unconcerned with tracking what their officers are doing in the field.

No one not lawmakers, the Department of Justice, or organizations like ours can know what to change without knowing how departments really are policing. Policing in the 21st century needs to take advantage of the information systems that we take for granted in so many other areas of public and private life.

Lacking solid information, officers in too many departments are managed and supervised based on gut instinct or intuition rather than objective evidence about an officer s performance. Personal affinities or the amorphous sense that an officer is a good guy or good gal leads supervisors to cut corners and cut breaks when it comes to accountability.

In the same way that many jurisdictions have adopted technological systems modeled after COMPSTAT, the pioneering and influential data system originating in New York City in the early 1990s, to guide officer deployment and crime prevention efforts[19], more need to adopt and proactively use data on how its officers are using force, making stops, and engaging with subjects in the field.

In most Department of Justice consent decrees and collaborative reform initiatives, a so-called Early Intervention System is a primary reform. The goal of these usually non-disciplinary systems is for departments to use objective data and information about what its officers are doing in the field in order to identify and respond proactively to performance trends that may suggest that an officer is at risk so that bad habits or bad apples can be addressed early and affirmatively.

The concept of an Early Intervention System is not new, and organizations like IACP and CALEA have advocated their use. Nonetheless, too many departments still lack the systems or, when they have them, fail to use them effectively. Supervisors often lack training on how to identify potential problems and how to interact with officers requiring intervention. In addition, too many departments focus the early intervention systems that they do have exclusively at line officers failing to examine whether supervisors and managers are living up to their own responsibilities.

IV. Discriminatory Policing Concerns

Within the communities where PARC works, we consistently hear from individuals that the weights and burdens of law enforcement are not equally shared. When they hear about the apparent choking death of a black man for peddling a few loose cigarettes, or the shooting of a black twelve-year-old two seconds after a police officer exited his patrol car, they wonder whether the outcomes might have been different if the subjects involved had looked different. Especially with respect to patterns of stops and detentions, empirical evidence supports the proposition that the practices of police in some areas are disproportionately affecting some of our communities more than others.[20]

The challenge for our police departments and our communities is to go beyond talking about the problem and looking for real-world solutions to addressing an issue that is clearly affecting the police-community relationship.

Abundant social science research has established that even individuals expressly committed to treating people equally may be affected by implicit biases or subconscious associations between Black, Latino, and some other historically minority populations and crime.[21] Individuals across professions and political ideologies have all been found prone to harbor subconscious associations between groups of individuals and crime.[22] Indeed, research indicates that nonwhite individuals also tend to exhibit implicit bias with respect to other non-white individuals.[23]

These implicit biases can particularly and unconsciously affect decisions in fast-moving situations the type of circumstances that police officers regularly encounter. Police officers may have subconscious biases in the same way that many people across various stations in life do, but the difficult job of police officers to make quick decisions based on limited information about previously unknown individuals heightens the risk that unconscious associations may have effects in the real world that drive distance between the police and our communities. This February, FBI Director James Comey called upon law enforcement to recognize this important fact.[24]

Forward-thinking departments are providing officers with clear strategies and tactics for attempting to minimize the effects of implicit bias by slowing situations down where feasible to ensure more time and space for identifying person-specific facts and by using intentional decision-making processes, again increasing officer and public safety.

Departments are also partnering with community organizations to provide training on procedural justice and fairness issues. Literature and life experience tells us that the *outcome* of an interaction matters less than an individual s sense of *how* he or she was treated.[25] Among individuals who get pulled over by a police officer, an individual s view of the incident correlates not with whether the officer gave them a ticket or not but, rather, with how fairly and equitably they believe that the officer treated them.

Just as ticket representatives for Southwest Airlines or customer service representatives at Federal Express receive training on problem-solving-oriented communication and are empowered to establish authentic, one-to-one relationships with the public,[26] patrol officers must feel empowered to find ways of making individuals across communities believe that the police are treating them not as a race, face, or place but as an individual.

CONCLUSION

In my ten years doing work with law enforcement agencies, I have encountered countless men and women who represent public service at its most competent, selfless, and laudable. However, even in healthy accountable police agencies where the interests and perspectives of the community are fully represented, officers may perform poorly. Some will make mistakes or bad decisions. To all of us and to the rank-and-file officers who execute their duties ably, fairly, and constitutionally accounts of officers engaging in misconduct are troubling. It can be tempting to conclude that nothing has changed in American policing and that nothing ever will.

Real reform is hard work. It rarely proceeds in straight lines. The true test, however, of whether we use this unique moment in American history is whether police agencies put in place the systems, policies, structures, and culture to manage for themselves the risk of unconstitutional policing. Departments must hold officers rigorously accountable through fair and transparent processes, critically analyze officer and departmental performance based on objective data, and proactively identify and seriously address performance issues and trends.

No police department is consigned to be only what it has been in the past. Organizational cultures change. New leadership can energize. Frayed relationships can mend. Old and rigid approaches can give way to dynamic innovation.

Modern American policing faces an era of unparalleled challenges. Too many communities view the police as them rather than us. The challenge that law enforcement agencies must embrace is to implement the kinds of tested, promising, and common-sense steps that might enhance public trust and legitimacy.

End Notes

[1] *See* Portland Police Bureau, Police Assessment Resource Center (last visited May 15, 2015), http://www.parc.info/portland/.

[2] *See* Thirty-Fourth Semiannual Report of Special Counsel, Los Angeles County Sheriff s Department (Aug. 2014), *Available at* http://static1.squarespace.com/static/5498b74ce 4b01fe317ef2575/t/54fc75b3e4b03edc59f8fd9b/1425831347689/34t h+Semiannual+Report.pdf.

[3] Bureau of Justice Statistics (BJS), *Local Police Departments, 2013: Personnel, Policies, and Practices* (May 2015), *available at* http://www.bjs.gov/content/pub/pdf/lpd13ppp.pdf.

[4] Joanna C. Schwartz, Myths and Mechanics of Deterrence: The Role of Lawsuits in Law Enforcement Decisionmaking, 57 U.C.L.A. L. Rev. 1023, 1027, 1023 (2010).

[5] 42 U.S.C. 14141.

[6] *Graham v. Connor*, 490 U.S. 387 (1989).

[7] *Scott v. Harris*, 127 S.Ct. 1769, 1777 (2007).

[8] U.S. Dept. of Justice, Civil Rights Division and U.S. Atty s Office, W.D. Wash. Investigation of Seattle Police Department at 14 (Dec. 16, 2011).

[9] *See, e.g.*, President s Task Force on 21st Century Policing, *Interim Report of the President s Task Force on 21st Century Policing* 21 (Mar. 2015) (recommending emphasis on de-escalation in policy and training); Utah Lawmakers Hold Study Session on Police Use of Force ; Matt Apuzzo, Police Rethink Long Tradition on Using Force, *N.Y. Times* (May 4, 2015) (discussing recent re-examination of police training in multiple departments).

[10] *United States v. City of Seattle*, 2:12-cv-01282-JLR, Dkt. No. 204-1 at 2, 8.

[11] Marc Santora, Mayor de Blasio Announces Retraining of New York Police, *N.Y. Times* (Dec. 4, 2014).

[12] Tony Larussa, W.Pa. police chiefs discuss use of force, de-escalation tactics, *Pittsburgh Tribune* (Jan. 8, 2015).

[13] Nat l Sheriffs Ass n & Treatment Advocacy Ctr., Justifiable Homicide by Law Enforcement Officers: What is the Role of Mental Illness at 6 (Sept. 2013).

[14] *See, e.g.*, Megan Pauly, How Police Officers Are (or Aren t) Trained in Mental Health, *Atlantic* (Oct. 11, 2013).

[15] International Association of Chiefs of Police, Improving Officer Response to Persons with Mental Illness and Other Disabilities: A Guide for Law Enforcement Leaders, *available at* http://www.theiacp.org/Portals/0/pdfs/IACP_Responding_to_MI.pdf; National Alliance on Mental Illness, CIT (last visited May 15, 2015), *available at* http://www2. nami.org/ Template.cfm?Section=CIT&Template=/ContentManagement/ContentDisplay.cfm&Content I D=150503.

[16] Merrick Bobb, et al, Police Assessment Resource Center, Review of National Police Oversight Models (2005).

[17] Heather Haddon, Newark Unveils Civilian Police-Review Board, *Wall Street Journal* (Apr. 30, 2015).

[18] Wesley Lowery, How many police shootings a year? No one knows, *Washington Post* (Sept. 8, 2014).

[19] See, e.g., Weisburd, et al., Reforming to Preserve: Compstat and Strategic Problem Solving *in* American Policing, 2 Criminology & Pub. Pol y 421, 422-23 (2003); Willis, et al., Making Sense of COMPSTAT: A Theory-Based Analysis of Organizational Change in Three Police Departments, 41 Law & Society Review 147, 148-49 (2007).

[20] *Floyd v. City of New York*, 1:08-cv-01034 at 21 (Aug. 12, 2013).

[21] *See* Kirwan Institute for the Study of Race and Ethnicity, State of the Science: Implicit Bias Review 2014 at 16, available at http://kirwaninstitute.osu.edu/wp-content/uploads/ 2014/03/2014-implicit-bias.pdf; *see generally* Thomas Gilovich, et al, *Heuristics and Biases: The Psychology of Intuitive Judgment* (2002); Daniel Kahneman, *Thinking, Fast and Slow* (2013).

[22] *See, e.g.*, Theodore Eisenberg & Sheri Lynn Johnson, Implicit Racial Attitudes of Death Penalty Lawyers, 53 DePaul L. Rev. 1539 (2004); Alexander R. Green, et al, Implicit Bias among Physicians and its Prediction of Thrombolysis Decisions for Black and White Patients, 22 Journal of Gen. Internal Medicine 1231 (2007); Tom Rudd, et al, Kirwan Inst., Racial Disproportionality in School Discipline (Feb. 2014), *available at* http:// kirwaninstitute.osu.edu/wp-content/uploads/2014/02/racial-disproportionality-schools-02.pdf.

[23] *See, e.g.*, Theodore R. Johnson, Black-on-Black Racism: The Hazards of Implicit Bias, *Atlantic* (Dec. 26, 2014) (noting that performance on implicit bias assessments reveal that black respondents subconsciously hold a slight preference for whites over blacks and harbor some subconscious biases with respect to blacks); Marcus Woo, How Science is Helping America Tackle Police Racism, *Wired* (Jan. 21, 2015) (Some studies found that even black people can have anti-black bias ... suggesting that the root of the bias isn t in any particular race, but in the prejudice and stereotype that s embedded throughout culture and society.).

[24] Remarks of James B. Comey at Georgetown Univ. (Feb. 12, 2015), *available at* http:// www.fbi.gov/news/speeches/hard-truths-law-enforcement-and-race.

[25] Rod K. Brunson & Jacinta M. Gau, Procedural justice and order maintenance policing: A study of inner-city young men s perceptions of police legitimacy, 27 Justice Quarterly 255 (2010).

[26] David E. Bowen & Edward E. Lawler III, Empowering Service Employees, MIT Sloan Management Review (July 15, 1995).

In: Police Use of Force …
Editor: Beverly Guzman
ISBN: 978-1-63484-557-1

Chapter 3

STATEMENT OF SUE RAHR, EXECUTIVE DIRECTOR, WASHINGTON STATE CRIMINAL JUSTICE TRAINING COMMISSION. HEARING ON "POLICING STRATEGIES FOR THE 21ST CENTURY"*

Public trust in American policing has been shaken across the nation by the images filling the airwaves beginning in Ferguson last summer and continuing with each new disturbing video that emerges every couple of weeks. These tragic incidents have sparked intense focus on the culture and practices of policing and has ignited a necessary national conversation. As we embark on this dialog it is critically important to consider the wide range of factors that impact the environment in which police operate and consider strategies that are most likely to increase public trust and improve public safety. I'd like to highlight two of the major factors.

The first factor is the absence of a national coherence in policing. We have 18,000 local police departments. That means 18,000 different cultures reflecting the policies and practices that are the product of 18,000 local governments serving communities with a diverse range of values and expectations. Agency size ranges from one-officer to more than 34,000. About half of the 18,000 agencies have less than 10 officers. All of those agencies operate in one of 50 states, each with their unique system of justice

* This is an edited, reformatted and augmented version of a statement presented May 19, 2015 before the House Judiciary Committee.

that dictates how criminal cases are initiated, processed, and adjudicated. Although many states mandate peace officer certification and standards for hiring and training, most states exert limited control over the routine operations of local police departments. Outside of Consent Decrees and the distribution or withholding of Federal funds, the influence the Federal Government has on local policing is also limited. Bottom line – there is no single description of police culture and practice in the United States. The environments and challenges faced by police departments vary widely, and control and oversight is almost exclusively local.

The second factor to consider is that police departments do not operate independently. In most cities, Police Chiefs are hired and fired by a Mayor, or another elected Municipal Executive. Most Sheriffs are elected by the voters they are sworn to serve and protect. When police exert control over citizens, they do so at the behest of officials elected by the people. Crime control strategies don't emerge in isolation. Nor do decisions about police accountability. Those decisions are made by independently elected local officials and Prosecutors. Too often the scrutiny of disturbing incidents begins and ends with the police department with little examination into those forces outside the agency that influence priorities and practices. The importance of a broader focus of inquiry was illustrated by the recent examination by the Department of Justice into the government practices in the City of Ferguson. The findings serve as a powerful example of the influence of governing forces outside of the police department itself.

Ideas for improving policing in the 21st Century need to be considered with these two important factors in mind. Most changes in policies and procedures must be adopted by local governments in order to be implemented. For example, a requirement to use body cameras must consider local and state laws related to the gathering, management, and disclosure of data as well as local and state laws protecting individual privacy. These changes will take time and require changes in state laws, with some barriers simply insurmountable.

There are, however, meaningful steps that can be taken at various levels of government, without changing laws. These steps will improve the culture of policing and expand police training in ways that contribute to increased public trust and improve public safety. The recommendations of the President's Task Force on 21st Century Policing contain a range of actions that can be implemented immediately, as well as longer term strategies.

In: Police Use of Force …
Editor: Beverly Guzman
ISBN: 978-1-63484-557-1

Chapter 4

FROM WARRIORS TO GUARDIANS: RECOMMITTING AMERICAN POLICE CULTURE TO DEMOCRATIC IDEALS*

Sue Rahr and Stephen K. Rice

> "In Plato's vision of a perfect society — in a republic that honors the core of democracy — the greatest amount of power is given to those called the Guardians. Only those with the most impeccable character are chosen to bear the responsibility of protecting the democracy." [1]

INTRODUCTION

Beginning in the 1960s, and more recently fueled by post 9-11 fear, American policing has slowly drifted away from Plato's vision of guardians and Socrates' view of guardian education as expressed in Plato's *Republic*. This view of guardian education is humanistic. It takes shape through criminal justice education that is not only vocational but also stresses ethics, theory and the nature of virtue.[2] As a profession, we have veered away from Sir Robert Peel's ideal, "the police are the people, and the people are the police," toward a culture and mindset more like warriors at war with the people we are sworn

---

* This is an edited, reformatted and augmented version of a paper, NCJ 248654, in the New Perspectives in Policing series, issued by the U.S. Department of Justice, National Institute of Justice, April 2015.

to protect and serve.[3] As a nation, we have tended to relinquish some of our sacred constitutional rights in favor of the perception of improved safety and security.[4] Constitutional rights are now viewed by some, including some police, as an impediment to the public safety mission. Sadly, many have forgotten that protecting constitutional rights is the mission of police in a democracy. As New York University law professor Stephen Schulhofer argues in a review of the Constitution and the police: "The future of individual liberties in this country depends on reinvigorating the system of vigorous checks and balances built into our Bill of Rights."[5] Such a call for reinvigoration of the civil religion of the state has strong historic precedent. As Lincoln argued before the Springfield Young Men's Lyceum in 1838:

> Let reverence for the laws, be breathed by every American mother to the lisping babe ... let it be taught in schools, in seminaries, and in colleges; let it be written in Primers, spelling books, and in Almanacs; let it be preached from the pulpit, proclaimed in legislative halls, and enforced in courts of justice. And, in short, let it become the political religion of the nation; and let the old and the young, the rich and the poor, the grave and the gay, of all sexes and tongues, and colors, and conditions, sacrifice unceasingly upon its altars.[6]

RECAPTURING THE FABRIC OF COMMUNITY

Despite two decades of aspiring to effective community policing, American law enforcement seems to have drifted off the course of building close community ties toward creating a safe distance from community members, in some cases substituting equipment and technology as the preferred means of gathering information about crime and addressing threats to public safety. In some communities, the friendly neighborhood beat cop — community guardian — has been replaced with the urban warrior, trained for battle and equipped with the accouterments and weaponry of modern warfare. Armed with sophisticated technology to mine data about crime trends, officers can lose sight of the value of building close community ties.

Largely stripped of a nuanced understanding of how communities operate, crime tracking and crime prediction software minimizes the utility of hard-earned intelligence provided by line officers who know their beats. After all, one's ability to glean meaning from algorithms is only as good as its sourcing: the accumulated body of knowledge of officers who have come to understand that there are few "straight lines" in policing — that (sometimes visceral) personto-person contact is typically not well-suited to statistical models.[7]

Most law enforcement leaders recognize that creating stronger human connections and community engagement will lead to improved public safety and more effective crime fighting. So how do we build the foundation of trust necessary to form a true partnership between the police and the people we serve? The research tells us that, despite three decades of falling crime rates — and improved training, technology and tactics — public trust in the police has not improved. Instead, empirical assessments of trust and confidence in the police have remained generally unchanged in recent years.[8]

It turns out that people don't care as much about crime rates as they do about how they are treated by the police.[9]

This phenomenon, known in academic circles as procedural justice, is regularly practiced and understood by effective and respected beat officers. The public knows it when they see it. But neither has likely heard of or used the term. Both beat officers and members of the public would describe procedural justice in action as being a good cop and doing the right thing.

More formally, Tom Tyler of Yale University explains that procedural justice focuses on perceived impartiality during interactions between police and the communities they serve, participation ("voice") from the public during these interactions, fairness, and consistency of treatment. Fairness relates to the protection of human rights and goals to include equal treatment, nondiscrimination, and nonpartisanship.[10]

As Tyler and colleagues explain, procedural justice relates directly to legitimacy. "If legal authorities exercise their authority fairly, they build legitimacy and increase both willing deference to rules and the decisions of the police and the courts and the motivation to help with the task of maintaining social order in the community."[11] Put another way, procedural justice refers to the set of procedures by which agents of social control such as police meet, or fail to meet, standards of consistency, suppression of bias, accuracy of information, mechanisms of rectification, and ethicality of standards in their interactions with the public.[12]

Few police leaders would disagree that community trust would improve if police officers routinely employed procedural justice during their interactions with the public. Training in these principles is under way in a number of locations around the nation.[13]

Elaborating on the specific behaviors of a good cop doing the right thing, the theory of procedural justice was simplified and operationalized for training street officers through a model developed in 2011 by then King County, Wash., Sheriff Sue Rahr (and first author of this paper), using the acronym LEED — Listen and Explain with Equity and Dignity. Using the LEED model, officers are trained to take the time to listen to people; explain what is going to happen and how the process works; explain why that decision was made so the equity of the decision is transparent; and leave the participants with their dignity intact.

Positive police contact facilitates public confidence.[14] People tell good cops what is going on in their neighborhoods and work with them to keep it safe. They view good cops as part of their community — one of the key distinguishing characteristics between cops with a guardian mindset and cops who operate with a warrior mindset. The guardian operates as part of the community, demonstrating empathy and employing procedural justice principles during interactions. The behavior of the warrior cop, on the other hand, leads to the perception of an occupying force, detached and separated from the community, missing opportunities to build trust and confidence based on positive interactions. Police leaders dedicated to establishing practices in their agencies based on procedural justice principles must ensure that their organizational culture is not in conflict with these same principles. As Stephen K. Rice and Karen Collins Rice explain, "Organizational systems, such as training, are nested within cultures that tend to go under-acknowledged but have tangible, and even visceral, impacts on the people working within them and their likelihood for embracing change."[15]

The current culture in some American law enforcement agencies tends toward the warrior mentality. The seeds of that culture are planted during recruit training, when some recruits are trained in an academy environment that is modeled after military boot camp, a model designed to produce a warrior ready for battle and ready to follow orders and rules without question. As Radley Balko points out in his noted book, *Rise of the Warrior Cop,* the warrior mentality threatens Fourth Amendment principles and casts the relationship between officers and citizens as a battle between "us" and "them." Balko pulls no punches in describing the Department of Justice under Attorney Generals William French Smith and Edwin Meese during the Reagan era:

> This would be a rough decade for the Symbolic Third Amendment [what Balko characterizes as strong American resistance to armies policing American streets]. Reagan's drug warriors were about to take aim at posse comitatus, utterly dehumanize drug users, cast the drug fight as a biblical

> struggle between good and evil, and in the process turn the country's drug cops into holy soldiers (p. 139).[16]

One of the many problems with the military boot camp model used in some academies is that it has little to do with the daily reality of policing. Whereas attention has been focused on the best span of control of supervisors to patrol officers,[17] in reality, few officers working the street have consistent or even regular supervision. No one is giving them orders or making decisions for them, and police executives cannot generate enough rules to cover the variety of situations they will face on the street. Plus, even if we were to create "enough" rules for officers to memorize, the effort conflicts with what cognitive science tells us about limits on working memory: young adults generally can keep no more than three to five items in mind at a time.[18] Given the realities of policing, critical thinking and decision-making, not memorization, should be a top goal of any training strategy.

Another, more insidious problem in a military-style academy is the behavior modeled by the academy staff. Those without power (recruits) submit without question to the authority of those who have power (academy staff). Rule violations are addressed by verbal abuse or physical punishment in the form of pushups and extra laps.

Day-to-day power differentials may be reinforced more subtly. As Chief David Couper relays on his more than 20 years in the Madison (Wisc.) Police Department:

> When I was introduced to the academy class that was already in training before I was appointed, the class stood at attention when I entered the room. In fact, I found that not only did they stand at attention when I entered, but that they did so for every supervisor who came into their class.
>
> A coercive, top-down leadership model had no place within a police department that was seeking highly educated people to come and join it. Some of the people we were trying to attract into a police career were currently in business, law, social work, or teaching. And most of them wouldn't choose to remain in a police department that ran like an 18th century British warship (p. 150).[19]

Upon graduation, we send our newly trained recruits out into the community — they finally have power. Despite the way they were treated during their training, we expect them to treat the powerless people they encounter in the community with dignity and respect. One example of requiring the most from the least experienced has been in New York, where for years newly credentialed officers have been placed in "Operation Impact" assignments in many of the city's most stressed neighborhoods.[20] Why are we then surprised when some officers treat both suspects and citizens with the disdain and detachment they saw modeled by those in power at the academy?

According to the lead author's experience working with police academies across the nation, much recruit training focuses on physical control tactics and weapons, with less attention given to communication and de-escalation skills. The reasoning for this approach is the sacred mantra of officer safety. We train relentlessly — as we should — in physical tactics for the high-risk, low-frequency attacks.[21] Less instructional attention is focused on human behavioral science. Yet seasoned cops and statistics tell us that the officer's intellect and social dexterity are often the most effective officer safety tools. For the sake of safety, voluntary compliance should be the primary goal in resolving conflict, with physical control reserved for those who present an immediate threat and cannot be managed any other way.

Don't misunderstand — we are not advocating a reduction in tactical training or equipment.

Officer safety is critical, and we must maintain vigorous instruction on physical control tactics and weapons. Those skills will always be necessary for dealing with individuals who refuse to comply and present an immediate threat. But we need to significantly increase the level of training and importance placed on communication skills and human behavioral science if we truly care about the safety of our officers. As Lt. Jim Glennon of the popular Calibre Press tactical training programs explains in his engaging book, *Arresting Communication,* "Mastering the skill of communication provides an officer with deep insight into what the public wants, who they are, and what their intentions might be."[22]

This leads to another great conundrum for leaders. A "physical control as last resort" maxim places immense importance on officer discretion, an orientation that can run counter to longstanding tendencies to regulate officer actions through operational control in the form of complex policies, rules and procedures.[23] To reduce the need for officers to use physical force, it may be necessary to increase their discretion and to trust their critical thinking and decision-making skills.[24]

What stands in the way of adopting a training model and culture that supports the development of critically thinking leaders with enhanced skills in managing human behavior? Tradition. Some perceive moving away from the boot camp model as coddling recruits, making them weak and diminishing officer safety. Worse yet, it could be perceived as "soft on crime," a political death knell to leaders since the 1960s.

However, there appear to be no clearly logical or evidence-based reasons that we should train police officers as we do soldiers. Although police officers wear uniforms and carry weapons, the similarity ends there. Their missions and rules of engagement are completely different. The soldier's primary mission is that of a warrior: to conquer. The rules of engagement are decided before the battle. The police officer's mission is that of a guardian: to protect. The rules of engagement evolve as the incident unfolds. In war, collateral damage is expected and accepted. Not so in policing. On the battlefield, the soldier acts on orders from a superior. In the community, the officer is the leader, rarely operating with the luxury of direct supervision.

Why aren't more police executives clamoring to train police officers to be more independent, critically thinking leaders? Because it is not consistent with the culture that exists in many American police agencies. The hierarchical, top-down control model remains the predominant structure both in the station and on the street. We do not encourage the rank and file to question authority. We cling to the belief that fear of punishment for rule violations leads to greater rule adherence and better police performance. Many still believe that an abundance of rules leads to fewer mistakes and greater accountability. Though well-intentioned, this style of leadership has the unintended but powerful consequence of conveying a distrust of officers by their leaders. It is no wonder that one of the hallmarks of law enforcement culture is the reciprocated distrust and disdain of police leadership by rank-and-file officers.

As David Bayley explains, "Authority is very much top-down, but perhaps for good reason. Policing needs to be accountable to law and morality, so supervisors double-down on discipline so as to minimize mistakes, they hope. Not only do officers not trust the community, but senior officers don't trust their officers. They don't know how to minimize mistakes except by minimizing discretion."[25]

This culture is mirrored on the street when police actions focus primarily on aggressive enforcement (zero tolerance) in the belief that fear of arrest is the best way to prevent criminal behavior. Just as it does internally, this overfocus on enforcement conveys the same level of distrust between those in power (police) and those under their authority (the public). Just as we measure internal organizational success by employee adherence to rules, we measure external operational success through crime rates and arrest statistics. We do both to the detriment of building trust and legitimacy, because they ignore what the research tells us and what the public and the rank and file tell us. Both the public and rank-and-file officers want to be treated fairly by those in authority. We should not be surprised that we end up with poor morale among our officers echoed by the lack of trust from the community.

CHANGING THE POLICE CULTURE FROM WARRIORS TO GUARDIANS

Perhaps it is time to reassess the predominant mindset of our profession, to change our culture — or rather recommit our culture — to democratic ideals. Perhaps it is time to revisit the wisdom of Plato and Sir Robert Peel and strive to become the trusted guardians of democracy. This will not be easy. In the first author's 35 years of experience, there are two things cops hate: the way things are, and change. When we add the emotional implications of changing culture, we must be prepared for strong resistance. That resistance will be intensified because we are challenging the very core of the warrior identity that many have embraced in the popular culture of policing. Furthermore, we are challenging the strict paramilitary organizational structure that is a hallmark of many police agencies. The challenge seems insurmountable.

There is good news. Change is afoot, and instructive examples are emerging around the country. One such transformation in training is taking place at the Washington State Criminal Justice Training Commission (WSCJTC). This transformation began in 2012, when Sue Rahr took over as the Executive Director. She brought with her the hard lessons from the street, the courts, and the political arena after serving 33 years with the King County Sheriff's Office, the last seven as the elected Sheriff. The following summary chronicles the transformation that occurred from 2012 to 2014 and continues today. This example is instructive for law enforcement leaders who are ready to transform their agencies from a culture of warriors to a culture of guardians.

TRANSFORMING POLICE TRAINING IN WASHINGTON STATE

The WSCJTC sets training standards, issues peace officer certifications, and conducts all mandated basic and advanced training for police, local corrections and a wide variety of other criminal justice system professionals. The Commission oversees the training of approximately 10,000 police officers and deputies from across the state, serving in 39 counties, 243 cities and a variety of tribal and state agencies. Each year, more than 600 police recruits receive 720 hours of basic training in programs that last 5 months. Figure 1 shows the courses and hours of training.

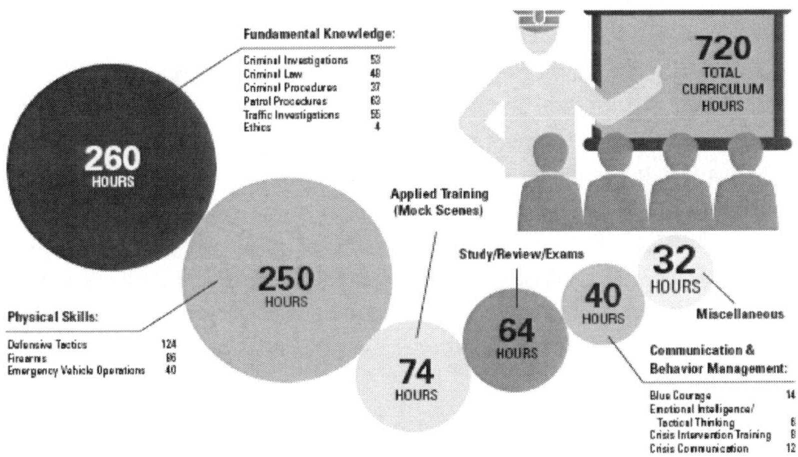

*Elements of the Communications and Behavioral Management training have been extensively integrated into the Fundamental Knowledge and Physical Skills blocks of training and must be demonstrated in Mock Scenes.

Figure 1. Basic Law Enforcement Academy Curriculum.

Before 2012, basic training was conducted according to a paramilitary "boot camp" model that employed a deterrence strategy to maintain discipline and control. Referred to as a "tune-up," starting the first day, training officers yelled at and berated new recruits for failing to complete drills designed to be impossible. Recruits were required to brace (salute) and remain silent whenever they encountered an academy staff member. Minor rule violations resulted in physical punishment in the form of extra pushups and running laps.

Despite the offering of behavioral and communications instruction in the classroom, the majority of the five-month training regimen emphasized physical skills training accompanied by a steady stream of fear-provoking stories about officers killed in the line of duty. Few classes effectively integrated communication skills and physical tactics. Physical control was emphasized over de-escalation. Conquering was emphasized over serving.

Most of the posters and visual aids in the classrooms carried themes related to deadly threats on the lives of officers. Skulls and crossbones were featured prominently. The lobby was decorated with display cases featuring the "tools of the trade." Legacy mementos from previous classes reflected a consistent theme of warriors, battles and survival. Noticeably absent from both the physical environment and curriculum was any reference to service and the noble and historical role of policing in a democracy.

What changed? The first change was the elimination of the protocol requiring recruits to brace. The new protocol requires recruits to initiate a conversation any time they come in contact with a staff member, taking care to make eye contact, show respect and address the person as "sir" or "ma'am."

The artificially imposed fear and humiliation from the "tune-up" day has been replaced by coaching. The standards for physical performance remain high, and training officers still push the recruits far beyond their physical limits. But, rather than screaming and berating the recruits, the training officers vigorously coach and encourage them to keep pushing. Instead of trying to instill a sense of fear, training officers strive to build a sense of camaraderie and pride for the success of the whole team.

The displays containing the "tools of the trade" in the main lobby were replaced by a large mural depicting the United States Constitution, framed by the following words in large relief: *"In These Halls ... Training the Guardians of Democracy,"* as shown in Figure 2. This theme has been replicated in several locations across the campus. Posters depicting the pride and honor of policing have been interspersed with the more traditional posters about officer safety. Speeches delivered at graduation ceremonies emphasize the nobility and higher purpose of policing and the distinction between the roles of warriors and guardians. During the first week, each recruit is presented a pocket-sized book containing the Constitution and the Declaration of Independence. A vigorous discussion about civil rights and the important role of policing in our democracy follows the presentation.

Behavioral and social science programs have been integrated into the 720-hour curriculum. Although intertwined, each of these programs has a distinct purpose that supports the others and contributes to better officer safety and improved public trust — two areas that, in the past, have been incorrectly viewed as mutually exclusive. They are:

- *Blue Courage.* Developed through a Bureau of Justice Assistance grant, this motivational program instills pride and supports values about the nobility of policing and the importance of maintaining physical, emotional and spiritual health. It has also been implemented at the Arizona Law Enforcement Academy and is currently being introduced to the rank and file at the New York Police Department and many other agencies across the nation.
- *Justice Based Policing.* This program, developed by the King County Sheriff's Office with funding from the Office of Community Oriented Policing Services, teaches the principles of procedural justice using the LEED model (Listen and Explain with Equity and Dignity).
- *Crisis Intervention Training.* This program teaches recruits to recognize behavioral cues associated with mental illness and traumatic brain injury and helps recruits develop strategies to de-escalate conflict and gain compliance. More than half of the "mock scenario" training and testing activities have been modified to include options and requirements for using crisis intervention techniques.
- *Tactical Social Interaction.* Academy personnel worked in partnership with Defense Advanced Research Program Administration (DARPA) researchers to create a program that teaches students specific, measurable actions that increase rapport between strangers and lead to positive social interaction. Although the program was developed to train Marine recruits how to conduct peacekeeping missions in foreign villages, it has shown great utility for police officers and is currently being adapted for both basic and in-service training.
- *"The Respect Effect."* Lessons from the book by Paul Meshanko about the neuroscience behind the acts of respect and disrespect to either motivate or antagonize[26] were integrated into the basic academy curriculum. At the same time, the entire WSCJTC staff completed the program as a demonstration of the effectiveness of this organizational strategy to begin cultural transformation.

What has not changed? Moving away from the "boot camp" model has not led to softening of the training. Recruits still must demonstrate a high level of proficiency in defensive tactics and firearms. In fact, additional firearms training time and tools have been added, and the defensive tactics program has been expanded to include more realistic and challenging scenarios.

Figure 2. A 6' x 9' Mural of the United States Constitution.

Discipline standards have not been relaxed. The use of formal titles and deference to senior officers and staff are still required. The changes made at the academy do not resemble previous experiments with "non-stress" academies, nor has the environment been changed to mirror a community college. The military protocols that have been retained (marching and formal flag ceremonies) are focused on patriotism and honor rather than power and submission. Behavioral strategies and decision-making have been integrated into physical control scenarios to better reflect the reality of policing.

A five-year longitudinal study of the effectiveness of the new training is now under way, having been launched in the fall of 2014. Researchers will follow cohorts of recruits for five years, conducting interviews and administering surveys at various intervals. The study is designed to determine if the guardian philosophy, the Blue Courage program and the Tactical Social Interaction program positively influence officers' attitudes about their job and the public. It will also measure whether or not officers trained under those programs are more likely to use crisis intervention strategies and de-escalation skills in the field than officers trained under the old warrior philosophy.

CONCLUSION

As this paper was being written, media images of officers atop armored personnel carriers, dressed in military fatigues and armed with rifles, have proven to be a powerful catalyst for vigorous discussion about the militarization of police in this country.[27] This debate should generate introspection by police leaders about cultures created within police agencies. This introspection should lead to a robust conversation with community members to assess whether police cultures reflect the values and expectations of the communities they serve.

AUTHOR NOTE

Sue Rahr is Executive Director of the Washington State Criminal Justice Training Commission and former King County Sheriff, Seattle, Wash. Stephen K. Rice, Ph.D., is Associate Professor of Criminal Justice at Seattle University.

The authors would like to thank Dr. David Bayley, Distinguished Professor Emeritus at the University at Albany, and Christine Cole, Vice President and Executive Director of the Crime and Justice Institute at Community Resources for Justice, for their thoughtful comments on earlier versions of this paper.

End Notes

1 Nila, Michael and Stephen R. Covey, *The Nobility of Policing,* West Valley City, Utah: Franklin Covey Publishing, 2008: 7.

2 See Holland, Kenneth, "Socrates: The First Criminal Justice Educator," *Criminal Justice Review,* 5(2) (1980): 1-4.

3 As a kind of "policing originalism," Sir Robert Peel has received newfound attention in his impact on New York Police Commissioner William Bratton. See Goldstein, Joseph and J. David Goodman, "A London Guide for 1 Police Plaza," *New York Times,* April 15, 2014, http:// www.nytimes.com/2014/04/16/nyregion/alondon-guide-for-1-police-plaza.html.

4 Within the context of homeland security and the risk of profiling, see, e.g., Rice, Stephen K. and William Parkin, "New Avenues for Profiling Research: The Question of Muslim Americans," in *Race, Ethnicity and Policing,* ed. S.K. Rice and M.D. White, New York: New York University Press, 2010.

5 Schulhofer, Stephen J., "The Constitution and the Police: Individual Rights and Law Enforcement," Washington *University Law Quarterly* 66 (1) (1988): 11.

[6] Lincoln, Abraham, "Address Before the Springfield Young Men's Lyceum," in *The Political Thought of Abraham Lincoln,* ed. R.N. Current, Indianapolis, Indiana: Bobbs-Merrill, 1967.

[7] For a useful conversation about the challenges and advantages of predictive policing software, see Vlahos, James, "The Department of Pre-Crime," *Scientific American,* January 2012.

[8] Tyler, T.R., "Trust and Legitimacy in the USA and Europe," *European Journal of Criminology* 8 (2011): 254-266.

[9] See Meares, Tracey L., *Rightful Policing,* New Perspectives in Policing Bulletin, Washington, D.C.: U.S. Department of Justice, National Institute of Justice, 2015. NCJ 248411; Meares Tracey L., Tom R. Tyler and Jacob Gardener, "Lawful or Fair? How Cops and Laypeople View Good Policing," Social Science Research Network, 2012, http://papers.ssrn.com/abstract=2116645 (last visited Nov. 13, 2014); Paternoster, Raymond, Ronet Bachman, Robert Brame, and Lawrence W. Sherman, "Do Fair Procedures Matter? The Effect of Procedural Justice on Spouse Assault," *Law and Society Review* 31 (1997): 163-197; Tyler, Tom R. and Yuen J. Huo, *Trust in the Law: Encouraging Public Cooperation With the Police and Courts,* New York: Russell Sage Foundation, 2002; Tyler, Tom R., "Enhancing Police Legitimacy," *Annals of the American Academy of Political & Social Science* 593 (2004): 84-99; Tyler, Tom R. and Jeffrey Fagan, "Legitimacy and Cooperation: Why Do People Help the Police Fight Crime in Their Communities?" *Ohio State Journal of Criminal Law* 6 (2008): 231; Tyler, Tom R. and Cheryl Wakslak, "Profiling and Police Legitimacy: Procedural Justice, Attributions of Motive, and Acceptance of Police Authority," *Criminology* 42 (2004): 253.

[10] See Hickman, Matthew J., "Democratic Policing: How Would We Know It If We Saw It?" in *Race, Ethnicity and Policing: New and Essential Readings,* ed. S. K. Rice and M.D. White, New York: New York University Press, 2010.

[11] See Tyler, Tom, Jonathan Jackson, and Ben Bradford, "Psychology of Procedural Justice and Cooperation," in *Encyclopedia of Criminology and Criminal Justice,* ed. G. Bruinsma and D. Weisburd, New York: Springer-Verlag, 2013.

[12] Leventhal, F.S., J. Karuza, Jr., and W.R. Fry, "Beyond Fairness: A Theory of Allocation Preferences," in *Justice and Social Interaction,* ed. G. Mikula, New York: Springer-Verlag, 1980: 167-218.

[13] One such effort is the Chicago Police Department's goal of training its 11,000 officers in procedural justice principles. See Fox, Aubrey, "Work in Progress: Can Police Officers Be Trained in Procedural Justice Principles?" *Augustus: The Latest Research* and *Commentary About Criminal Justice Reform,* Apr. 16, 2013.

[14] Bradford, Ben, Jonathan Jackson, and Elizabeth A. Stanko, "Contact and Confidence: Revisiting the Impact of Public Encounters With the Police," *Policing and Society: An International Journal of Research and Policy* 19(1) (2009): 20-46.

[15] Rice, Stephen K. and Karen Collins Rice, "How to Change the Culture of the Seattle Police Department," *Seattle Times* (June 20, 2014), http://seattletimes.com/html/opinion/2023892606_stephenkarencollinsriceoped policereform23xml. html.

[16] Balko, Radley, *Rise of the Warrior Cop: The Militarization of America's Police Forces,* New York: Public Affairs Books, 2013.

[17] See Johnson, O'Ryan, "Police Supervisors Push Marty Walsh to Add 40 to Staff," *Boston Herald,* May 24, 2014, http://bostonherald. com/news_opinion/local_coverage/2014/05/police_supervisors_push_marty_walsh_to_ add_40_to_staff (accessed May 25, 2014).

[18] See Cowan, Nelson. "The Magical Mystery Four: How Is Working Memory Capacity Limited, and Why?" *Current Directions in Psychological Science* 19 (2010): 51-57.

[19] Couper, D.C., *Arrested Development: A Veteran Police Chief Sounds Off About Protest, Racism, Corruption and the Seven Steps Necessary to Improve Our Nation's Police,* Indianapolis, Indiana: Dog Ear Publishing, 2011.

[20] The tide may be shifting, however. As New York Police Commissioner William Bratton explained recently, "I want to change the dynamic of kids coming out of the academy and immediately being put into Operation Impact assignments, where they really have an almost single-minded focus and really don't get a full flavor of the job." Goodman, J. David, "Bratton Says Rookies' Role in Anticrime Effort Will End." *The New York Times,* Feb. 1, 2004, http://www.nytimes. com/2014/02/01/nyregion/bratton-tells-chiefshell-stop-sending-rookies-to-high-crime-areas. html (accessed May 25, 2014).

[21] Methodologically, this "high risk, low frequency" operational environment has been assessed by way of "danger ratios" and similar tools (see, e.g., Garner, Joel and Elizabeth Clemmer, *Danger to Police in Domestic Disturbances,* Washington, D.C.: U.S. Department of Justice, National Institute of Justice, 1986. Garner and Clemmer's formula uses the ratio of violent incidents divided by the total police activity in the area of focus).

[22] Glennon, Jim, *Arresting Communication: Essential Interaction Skills for Law Enforcement,* Villa Park, Illinois: LifeLine Training, 2010: 35.

[23] See Alpert, Geoffrey P. and William C. Smith, "Developing Police Policy: An Evaluation of the Control Principle," *American Journal of Police* 13 (1994): 1.

[24] For an excellent review of cutting-edge research on decision-making and problem-solving, see Brockman, John (ed.), *Thinking: The New Science of Decision-Making, Problem-Solving, and Prediction,* New York: Harper Collins, 2013. Of particular relevance to policing is *Thinking's* discussion of the smart heuristics that expert performers use to make good decisions. As Brockman explains, "In order to make good decisions in an uncertain world, one sometimes has to ignore information. The art is knowing what one doesn't have to know" (p. 40).

[25] Bayley, David, personal correspondence, June 15, 2014.

[26] Meshanko, Paul, *The Respect Effect: Using the Science of Neuroleadership to Inspire a More Loyal and Productive Workplace,* Columbus, Ohio: McGraw-Hill Education, 2013.

[27] Militarization of the police within the context of Ferguson has received explicit attention. See, e.g., http://www. msnbc.com/andrea-mitchell-reports/watch/ police-militarization-adds-to-fergusonchaos-319148099539.

In: Police Use of Force …
Editor: Beverly Guzman
ISBN: 978-1-63484-557-1

Chapter 5

FEDERAL TACTICAL TEAMS*

Nathan James

SUMMARY

In 2014 and 2015, reports of Special Weapons and Tactics (SWAT) teams used by law enforcement agencies in allegedly questionable raids or in what appeared to be aggressive responses to public disturbances generated interest among policymakers in federal tactical teams. There is no single source for data on federal tactical teams. The Congressional Research Service (CRS) surveyed federal agencies with law enforcement personnel to collect basic information on any tactical teams they maintain.

The number of tactical teams has proliferated among American law enforcement since the first SWAT team was formed by the Los Angeles Police Department in the 1960s. Research has shown that most law enforcement agencies now have a tactical team. Data also show that these teams are being deployed more frequently. As the acronym SWAT implies, such teams are deployed against particularly dangerous criminals and in challenging situations. This report provides baseline data on federal tactical teams.

Thirteen agencies that responded to a CRS questionnaire reported having 271 tactical teams. The federal-wide number is almost certainly higher, as the U.S. Park Police and thc U.S. Capitol Police did not respond to CRS. Nearly

* This is an edited, reformatted and augmented version of a Congressional Research Service. publication, No. R44179, dated September 3, 2015.

all tactical teams (93%) are in agencies that are a part of the Department of Justice (213 teams) or the Department of Homeland Security (39 teams). A small proportion (2%) of all federal law enforcement officers serve on tactical teams, and for most of those who do, it is an ancillary duty. Data collected by CRS also suggest a 90% increase from 1,171 to 2,227 deployments by federal tactical teams between FY2005 and FY2014.

There are several issues policymakers might consider should Congress take up legislation or conduct oversight related to how federal agencies use tactical teams. Potential legislative issues include the following:

- Is there a need to collect data on federal tactical teams? If so, what data should be collected, who should collect it, and how frequently should it be disseminated?
- Should Congress place limits on when tactical teams can be deployed?
- Should federal tactical operations be centralized in one agency?
- Should federal tactical officers be required to participate in a basic training course that focuses on the skills necessary for participating on a tactical team? Should there be universal standards for the ongoing training of tactical officers?

Potential oversight issues include the following:

- What types of operations are federal agencies conducting with their tactical teams?
- Where are tactical officers receiving their training? What type of training are they receiving?
- How are decisions made about when to deploy tactical teams?
- What are the results of tactical operations?

Several recent incidents in which Special Weapons and Tactics (SWAT) teams were reportedly used in questionable raids or in aggressive responses to public disturbances generated interest among policymakers in federal tactical teams (e.g., SWAT, special response, emergency response, or active shooter teams).[1] Legislation has been introduced in the current Congress that would require the Government Accountability Office (GAO) to issue an annual report on federal tactical teams.[2] Other legislation has been introduced that would require the Department of Justice (DOJ) to collect, analyze, and publish data on federal, state, and local tactical teams.[3]

As indicated by the requirements that would be put in place by legislation introduced in the current Congress, there is a dearth of data on federal tactical teams. The Congressional Research Service (CRS) surveyed federal agencies with law enforcement personnel[4] to collect basic information on any tactical teams they maintain, and the results are presented in this report. The report provides a brief overview of the development of tactical teams at the state and local level and the concerns raised by their expansion. It then discusses the composition of these teams in the federal government. It concludes with a discussion of potential issues for policymakers to consider if they take up legislation or conduct oversight related to how the federal government uses tactical teams.

WHAT IS A SWAT TEAM?

While there is no universal definition of what constitutes a SWAT team (or police paramilitary units (PPUs), as they are sometimes called in related academic literature)[5] the National Tactical Officers Association defines a SWAT team as a "designated law enforcement team, whose members are recruited, selected, trained, equipped and assigned to resolved critical incidents involving a threat to public safety which would otherwise exceed the capabilities of traditional law enforcement first responders and/or investigative units."[6] Further, "[t]he primary characteristics of SWAT [teams] that distinguishes it from other units is the focus of effort. SWAT teams are focused on tactical solutions, as opposed to other functions, such as investigations."[7]

A scholar on police militarization notes that PPUs can be distinguished from traditional police in the following ways:

- PPUs are equipped with an array of militaristic equipment and technology (e.g., H&K MP5 submachine guns, semi-automatic shotguns, M16 assault rifles, and sniper rifles).
- PPUs have an array of "less-than-lethal" weapons and technology that they use when conducting "dynamic entries" (e.g., "flash-bang" grenades, tear gas, bean bag guns, battering rams, hydraulic door-jamb spreaders, and armored personnel carriers).

- PPU organizational structures are modeled after the military and foreign special operations teams. They train collectively under a military command structure and discipline.
- PPUs are traditionally deployed for "high-risk" situations. High-risk situations are those that require a squad of police officers who are trained as use-of-force specialists.[8]

The Debate over SWAT Teams

The debate about the proliferation and use of SWAT teams is framed by law enforcement's desire to protect their own from death or bodily injury in hazardous situations and concerns over how and when law enforcement uses force against citizens. A scholar on police militarization summarizes the debate over the expansion of PPUs as such:

> To many people, even among academics, the military model represents constraint, discipline, honor, control, competence, and even a type of patriotism. To others it stands for tyranny, state violence, human rights abuses, war, and an ideology which stresses that problems are best handled by technologized state force. Some will see the rise and normalization of PPUs as a necessary and rational approach to today's crime, gang, and drug problems; others will view it as bureaucracy building and as evidence of a government in crisis moving towards a police state.[9]

Theories About the Proliferation of SWAT Teams

Some scholarly speculation has addressed the forces driving the expansion of PPUs. For example, the "war on drugs" and the "war on terror" may have given rise to the militarization of police by providing a crisis in which law enforcement could expand its size, scope, and power.[10] The "war on drugs" and the "war on terror" may have increased demands from the public for the government to do something about the crises.[11] Additionally, cooperation between the military and law enforcement as they conducted joint operations in the "wars" may have contributed to the expansion of PPUs.[12] Finally, technological improvements have lowered the cost for law enforcement to adopt military technology. Technology that was once exclusively used by the military—such as facial recognition systems, thermal imaging, and satellite monitoring—can now be used by law enforcement.[13]

BACKGROUND ON HOW SWAT TEAMS ARE USED BY STATE AND LOCAL LAW ENFORCEMENT

This section provides a brief review of the literature on SWAT teams. To date the literature on this topic has focused exclusively on state and local law enforcement's tactical teams. The purpose of this literature review is twofold. First, it provides an overview of the findings of research that might have generated interest among policymakers in how federal law enforcement agencies are using their tactical teams. Second, it provides a basis for the questions submitted to federal agencies with law enforcement personnel by CRS to inquire about their tactical teams.

SWAT teams started to appear in the late 1960s. A series of high-profile incidents, such as a sniper attack at the University of Texas-Austin and the Watts riots in Los Angeles, raised concerns that regular law enforcement was not capable of responding effectively to some violent episodes.[14] As a result, some law enforcement agencies started to form SWAT teams as a way to handle extraordinarily dangerous situations.[15] From the start, tactics employed by SWAT teams were designed to protect the safety of officers, the public, victims, and offenders.

The Los Angeles Police Department created the first SWAT team in the late 1960s. Since then PPUs have proliferated to the point that most law enforcement agencies now have them. A 1996 survey of law enforcement agencies serving jurisdictions of 50,000 or more people found that approximately 89% of responding agencies reporting having a PPU in that year, compared to 59% in 1982.[16] Another 1996 survey found that for law enforcement agencies serving jurisdictions of between 25,000 and 50,000 people, 65% of responding agencies reported having a PPU in that year,[17] compared to only 20% at the beginning of 1980.[18] Of note, it does not appear that any agency or organization regularly collects and reports data on tactical teams; therefore, the surveys of PPUs conducted in 1996 provide the most complete data currently available.

Data show that PPUs were deployed with increasing frequency during the 1980s and 1990s. There was a reported 1,400% increase in the total number of PPU deployments between 1980 and 2000 (an estimated 45,000 PPU deployments in 2000 compared to an average of 3,000 deployments in 1980).[19]

Data from an American Civil Liberties Union (ACLU) study also suggest that racial minorities are more likely to be the target of PPU raids.[20] In its study of PPU raids conducted by 20 law enforcement agencies in 11 states, the ACLU found that 39% of people affected by PPU raids were black, 11% were Latino, and 20% were white.[21] Data on the race of affected people were not available in 30% of the cases. The ACLU found that minorities were more likely to be affected by PPU drug raids; 61% of all people affected by drug raids were minorities.[22] Minorities were also more likely to be affected by PPUs raids for serving search warrants; 54% of all people affected by search warrant raids were minorities.[23] This stands in contrast to raids where whites were more likely to be affected. In those cases, PPUs were more likely to be deployed for situations involving active shooters, barricaded suspects, or hostage situations.

The increase in the number of PPU deployments might not be a concern if it were related to PPUs' essential functions—namely reactive deployments of high-risk specialists for particularly dangerous events in progress, such as hostage, sniper, or terrorist situations. However, there is concern that PPU deployments are increasing because of "mission creep." Data show that nearly 80% of current PPU deployments are for proactive drug raids or to execute search warrants.[24] In addition, it has been reported that PPUs are increasingly being used to conduct routine patrol work in crime "hot spots."[25] Such uses seem to veer away from the extraordinarily violent or dangerous situations for which PPUs were created.

While it appears that in recent years police have deployed PPUs more frequently and used them more expansively, it is unclear whether this has led to increased violent confrontations between police and the people they serve. Two researchers who conducted a national study of PPUs in law enforcement agencies with more than 50 sworn officers reported that there is a high degree of professionalism in how PPUs conduct their operations. They concluded that members of PPUs conduct themselves in a manner consistent with their training and that they do not frequently use deadly force to resolve situations.[26] The researchers note that "officers took suspects under fire in just 342 of the tens of thousands of operations they undertook."[27] However, they also note that there were an unacceptably high number of accidental firearms discharges reported during PPU operations.[28]

Even though some research suggests that PPUs conduct their missions with a high level of professionalism, few studies have probed the effect that increased reliance on PPUs may have on public trust of police. Most police departments have standards in place that provide for PPU deployment for hostage taking, active shooters, barricaded suspects, emergency scenarios, or serving "high-risk" warrants (though what constitutes a high-risk scenario is largely left to the discretion of the officers involved).[29] Research from the ACLU raises questions about whether there is enough oversight of how PPUs are deployed. The ACLU reports that state or local authorities conduct little oversight of how law enforcement agencies are using PPUs.[30] In addition, it appears that many law enforcement agencies do not collect consistent data on PPU deployments—and they are reluctant to share it when they do.[31]

Professionalism depends on training, but training appears to be highly localized, varying from agency to agency. Training provides PPUs with opportunities to identify weak points in their capabilities, such as conditions that lead to the accidental discharge of firearms, and make efforts to strengthen them. A large majority (81%) of teams reported training between 8 and 20 hours per officer per month.[32] Also, officers on part-time PPUs tend to train less than officers on full-time teams.[33] A national study of PPUs concluded that PPUs that are "currently on the lower end of the training time distribution should seek to increase the time they devote to training. Because the potential costs associated with [PPU] failure are quite high—the unnecessary loss of life and limb, as well as the potential fallout from [those actions]—[PPUs] should be encouraged to undertake the sort of rigorous training that will permit them to identify and correct problems before they lead to operational failure."[34]

As suggested above, there is concern that the reported normalization of PPUs is changing the face of policing in the United States and the relationship between law enforcement agencies and the citizens they serve. Some argue that militarized training and equipment used by PPUs can promote a soldier's mentality among police officers, which can act as a barrier to police-community ties by fostering an "us versus them" attitude.[35] Also, a militaristic ideology and organization may be adverse to democratic approaches to overseeing and administering police functions.[36] The military model arguably places a greater emphasis on the crime-fighting role of police and a warlike approach to solving social problems, such as drug use or gangs.[37]

It has also been argued that law enforcement agencies are integrating PPUs into their community policing strategies. Research on SWAT teams indicates that many law enforcement agencies believe they play an important role in community policing strategies.[38] In addition, scholars argue that "community policing" is just a way for law enforcement agencies to present their old ways in a new package. Two scholars note, "[law enforcement agencies] are managing to reconstitute their image away from the citizen-controller paradigm based in the autonomous legal order and towards a more comforting Normal Rockwell image—police as kind, community care-takers."[39] They contend that community policing is more about police transforming their image rather than the substance of their work.

As previously noted, the literature on PPUs has focused on their use by state and local law enforcement. Any of the issues raised in the literature are specific to state and local law enforcement PPUs, but they might serve as a basis for inquiry about how federal agencies use their PPUs. The lack of literature on federal tactical teams posed a barrier for CRS to respond to congressional inquiries about the topic. As such, CRS conducted its own inquiry into which federal agencies have tactical teams and how they are used. The report now turns to the results of CRS's study.

FEDERAL TACTICAL TEAMS

CRS received data from 65 of the 71 federal agencies that employ law enforcement personnel.[40] Of the 65 responding agencies, 13 reported that they had tactical teams:[41]

- Federal Bureau of Investigation (FBI);
- Bureau of Prisons (BOP);
- Drug Enforcement Administration (DEA);
- U.S. Marshals Service (USMS);
- Bureau of Alcohol, Tobacco, Firearms, and Explosives (ATF);
- Customs and Border Protection (CBP);
- Immigration and Customs Enforcement (ICE);
- U.S. Secret Service;
- Bureau of Diplomatic Security;
- Pentagon Force Protection Agency;
- National Institutes of Health (NIH) Police;
- National Nuclear Safety Administration (NNSA); and
- National Aeronautic and Space Administration (NASA) Police.

Number of Tactical Teams

These 13 agencies reported having a total of 271 tactical teams (Table B-1). Some 145 of those (54%) were part of the Bureau of Prisons (BOP). Nearly all tactical teams (93%) were in agencies that are part of the Department of Justice (DOJ, 213 teams) or the Department of Homeland Security (DHS, 39 teams).

While the term Special Weapons and Tactics (SWAT) has become synonymous with tactical teams, many federal agencies do not refer to their teams as SWAT (Table B-2). The FBI was the only federal agency that reported having SWAT teams. Many federal agencies refer to their tactical teams as Emergency Response Teams (ERTs) or Special Response Teams (SRTs).

Number of Tactical Officers

A small proportion of all federal law enforcement officers serve on tactical teams. Responding agencies reported employing 145,045 law enforcement officers (Table B-1). Of those, 2,888 (2%) were assigned to work on a tactical team. The data show that most law enforcement officers serve on tactical teams as an ancillary duty; 906 (31%) were assigned to a team full-time. The DEA, Bureau of Diplomatic Security, Pentagon Force Protection Agency, and NNSA were the only agencies that reported that all of their tactical officers served full-time. All members of the FBI's Hostage Rescue Team (HRT) and CBP's Border Patrol Tactical Unit (BORTAC) serve full-time. Nearly all (93%) of the agents who serve on CBP's SRT serve full-time.

The Role of Federal Tactical Teams

In general, federal tactical teams can be divided into two classes. There are tactical teams that support law enforcement officers who investigate and respond to criminal activity (i.e., the CBP, ICE, FBI, ATF, USMS, and DEA, though the DEA reported that their teams do not operate domestically), and there are tactical teams that provide support to law enforcement officers who are responsible for providing security for federal property and/or personnel (i.e., the BOP, Secret Service, Pentagon Force Protection Agency, Bureau of

Diplomatic Security, NIH Police, NASA Police, and NNSA). **Table B-3** provides descriptions of the roles for federal tactical teams.

It appears that many of the tactical teams that support law enforcement agencies whose primary role is to provide security would not conduct operations off federal property. For example, the BOP's tactical teams most likely would not conduct operations outside of a federal prison. This would make these tactical teams somewhat different that PPUs operated by state and local law enforcement and tactical teams operated by federal law enforcement agencies with investigatory responsibilities in that they would not conduct operations in people's homes or on private property. However, while on federal property their functions and operations resemble those of a regular PPU.

Within these two broad classes, federal tactical teams have a variety of responsibilities. In general, agencies appear to deploy their tactical team(s) in situations that they feel are beyond the abilities of their regular law enforcement personnel or in instances where a higher level of security needs to be provided. Responses from the 13 agencies that reported having tactical teams show that the teams are deployed for a variety of reasons (**Table B-6**). Some of these reasons are consistent with how SWAT teams are used by local law enforcement agencies: serving high-risk warrants or used for high-risk apprehensions (six agencies); responding to active shooters (four); rescuing hostages (five); responding to terrorist attacks (four); and responding to barricaded suspects (five).

However, agencies also identified reasons why their tactical teams would be deployed that are related to the unique jurisdiction of some federal law enforcement agencies. For example, seven agencies indicated that they would deploy their teams to provide protection for high-risk targets such as government officials or foreign dignitaries. Four agencies reported that they would deploy their teams to provide security at special events. Also, the U.S. Marshals Service reported that its tactical team can be used to apprehend fugitives, provide witness security, or transport high-risk or dangerous prisoners. The NIH Police and the NNSA use their tactical teams to provide security for sensitive materials, such as nuclear material. The DEA's tactical teams conduct counter-drug operations overseas and provide assistance to foreign governments' drug enforcement agencies. The BOP deploys its tactical teams to respond to institutional disturbances.

In addition, four agencies reported that they deploy their tactical teams to help respond in cases of natural disasters; three agencies reported deploying their teams to conduct high-risk surveillance; four agencies reported they would deploy their teams to respond to terrorist attacks; and two agencies would deploy their teams to provide support to undercover operations.

Tactical Team Training

Agencies reported that officers who serve on tactical teams receive their training from a variety of sources, and many indicated that their officers receive training from more than one source.

- A majority of agencies that reported having tactical teams (11 of 13) provided some training to their tactical officers in-house.
- Two agencies reported that their tactical officers receive some training through the Federal Law Enforcement Training Center (FLETC).
- Four agencies reported that their tactical officers receive some training from outside organizations or experts such as the National Tactical Officers Association.
- Two agencies reported that their tactical officers receive training from other law enforcement agencies.

The number of reported training hours for tactical teams ranged from 3 to 160 hours per month (see **Table B-4**). The DEA reported that its tactical teams train 160 hours per month (when they are not deployed), which is a clear outlier. The next highest number of training hours per month was 80 for the FBI's Hostage Rescue Team. The average amount of training hours per month for all 13 responding agencies was 36. The median number of training hours was 22 hours per month.

On average, full-time tactical teams train more frequently (65 hours per month) than part-time teams (19 hours per month). Even if the DEA is excluded, full-time teams train an average of 41 hours per month.

When Were Tactical Teams Established?

The earliest that any responding agencies reported establishing their tactical teams was 1971 (the USMS Special Operations Group and the Secret Service Counter Sniper Branch). The majority of tactical teams (232 of the 271) were established prior to 1990 (see Table B-5). It was reported that the 39 remaining tactical teams were founded in 1996 or later; two-thirds of these were DHS tactical teams. The most recently established tactical teams are all a part of DHS.[42] ICE established 11 of its 17 Homeland Security Investigation SRTs and all 8 of its Enforcement and Removal Operations SRTs between 2005 and 2013. CBP established its Office of Field Operations SRT in 2007.

Tactical Team Deployments

Eleven of the 13 agencies that reported having tactical teams were able to provide data on how many times those teams were deployed each fiscal year from FY2005 to FY2014 (see Table B-7). However, two agencies, the USMS and the NASA Police, only provided an annual average number of deployments. Also, three agencies submitted data for fewer than 10 fiscal years: CBP (FY2007-FY2014),[43] ICE (FY2006-FY2014), and the NIH Police (FY2014).[44] Figure 1 presents data on the number of deployments for federal tactical teams for the past 10 fiscal years.

The data presented in Figure 1 must be interpreted with caution. Not all agencies were able to provide data on the number of times their teams deployed. As noted, two agencies only provided an average annual number of deployments, and not all responding agencies provided data for each of the 10 fiscal years. Also, the data are limited to the past 10 fiscal years. So while the data suggest that tactical team deployments have been increasing, it is possible that the reported number of deployments in FY2005 was a historical low and the number of reported deployments in the later fiscal years is a return to historical norms. As such, the data can provide some insight into the trend in the number of federal tactical team deployments over the past 10 fiscal years, but the data do not show the *actual* number of deployments each fiscal year.

Overall, the number of federal tactical team deployments appears to be increasing. The total number of reported deployments increased 90% between FY2005 and FY2014. Five agencies— the FBI, ATF, ICE, CBP, and Pentagon Force Protection Agency—accounted for more than 90% of the annual number of tactical team deployments during this period. The FBI accounted for the highest *number* of deployments each year, though their proportion of the total number of deployments steadily decreased from 72% in FY2005 to 48% in FY2014. This was largely the result of the ATF, CBP, ICE, and the Pentagon Force Protection Agency deploying their tactical teams with greater frequency. FBI deployments increased from 840 to 1,065 between FY2005 and FY2014.

During the same period the number of deployments by the Pentagon Force Protection Agency increased from 144 to 255. ICE deployments increased from 134 in FY2006 to 398 in FY2014, while CBP deployments increased from 2 in FY2007 to 225 in FY2014.

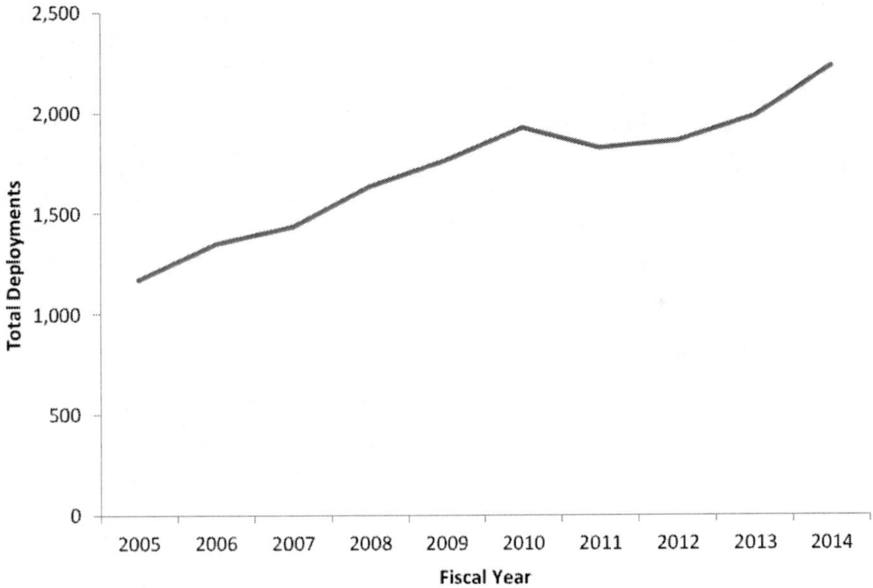

Source: Data collected as a part of CRS's survey of federal tactical teams.

Notes: The USMS and the NASA police only reported the average annual number of deployments over the entire time period for their tactical teams. The average number of deployments was used each fiscal year when calculating the total number of deployments. For example, the USMS reported that on average its Special Operations Group (SOG) deployed 28 times each fiscal year, so when calculating the total of tactical team deployments each fiscal year it was assumed that the USMS SOG deployed 28 times each fiscal year.

Figure 1. Estimated Number of Deployments for Responding Federal Tactical Teams, FY2005-FY2014.

ATF and ICE provided data on how their tactical teams were deployed in FY2014. The data show that the tactical teams for these two agencies were primarily used to serve warrants. Seven out of every eight deployments for the ATF SRT were to execute a warrant or to support undercover operations. Approximately 85% of the ICE SRT deployments were for serving warrants, supporting undercover operations, and conducting high-risk transports. These data suggest that like PPUs maintained by state and local law enforcement, federal tactical teams are being "normalized" in regular law enforcement operations. That is to say, they are being used for operations beyond those for which PPUs were originally established: responding to active shooters, barricaded suspects, or hostage situations.

It is not exactly clear why there may have been an increase in the number of tactical team deployments. One explanation could be that there are more tactical teams, given that DHS has established many of its teams since 2005. Another could be that federal agencies have gotten better at tracking the number of times their tactical teams deploy. Yet another could be that the missions of the teams have expanded or federal agencies have chosen to use the teams in more expansive ways under existing missions. Data presented above suggest this might be part of the explanation. Though they are only for two agencies in one fiscal year, it appears that federal tactical teams are being used in ways other than responding to high-risk situations. The data available for FY2014 deployments suggest that serving warrants is an important role for federal tactical teams. While the FBI did not provide data on how their SWAT teams and the HRT were deployed in FY2014, it reported to CRS that the vast majority of SWAT team deployments are in support of FBI investigations serving high-risk arrest and search warrants.

ISSUES FOR CONGRESS

There are several issues related to federal tactical teams Congress might consider. Some of the issues are legislative, some are related to oversight.

Potential Legislative Issues

Potential legislative issues might include the following:

- Is there a need to collect data on federal tactical teams? If so, what data should be collected, who should collect it, and how frequently should it be disseminated?
- Should Congress place limits on when tactical teams can be deployed?
- Should federal tactical team operations be centralized in one agency?

- Should federal tactical officers be required to participate in a basic training course that focuses on the skills necessary for participating on a tactical team? Should there be standards for the ongoing training for tactical officers?

Collecting Data on Federal Tactical Teams

As discussed at the beginning of this report, there does not appear to be any single source for a list of federal agencies that maintain tactical teams, let alone a source for more detailed data such as how many officers serve on those teams, how frequently they are deployed, the type of missions they undertake, and the result of those missions. One issue policymakers might consider is whether a federal agency should be designated to collect and disseminate data on federal tactical teams. For example, the Bureau of Justice Statistics (BJS) conducts a quadrennial survey of federal agencies to collect data on federal law enforcement personnel.[45] It might be that BJS could expand its efforts to collect data on federal tactical teams.

Policymakers might also consider how frequently the data should be reported and collected relative to the effort required to collect the data. For example, Congress might want data on federal tactical teams more frequently than once every four years. However, if an agency like BJS were required to collect and report data annually, it might have to dedicate more resources toward those efforts.

Another issue Congress might consider is what type of data should be collected, especially if they were made public. While collecting and reporting data on federal tactical team operations could promote more transparency—and there have been calls for more transparency related to tactical teams[46]—law enforcement might not want to make all details about tactical team deployments public.

Limits on Deployments

Some policymakers might consider whether Congress should place limits on when federal agencies can deploy their tactical teams. As noted earlier, the literature on PPUs operated by state and local law enforcement agencies indicates that their missions have expanded to include operations outside of the original intent for the formation of these teams, namely to respond to extraordinarily violent or dangerous situations. Data collected by CRS suggests that federal tactical teams are engaging in some of the same kind of operations (e.g., serving warrants or supporting undercover operations). The expansion of tactical team operations into more traditional policing responsibilities is sometimes referred to as "mission creep." Passing legislation that requires federal agencies to deploy their teams only in certain circumstances could be one way for Congress to limit "mission creep."

While it might be justifiable to try to place legislative limits on when a tactical team could be deployed, this could limit the discretion of law enforcement agencies to deploy their teams in situations where it might be appropriate to do so. It might be that law enforcement personnel on the scene are the best suited to make determinations about whether a tactical team should be deployed. There might be questions about whether policymakers could legislate all of the situations under which federal agencies would be allowed to deploy their teams. Also, if Congress wishes to restrict when federal agencies can deploy their tactical teams, it would probably require legislators to define "tactical team." If Congress were to do so, federal agencies may see an incentive to reorganize their teams to avoid restrictions on how and when they are used.

Rather than placing statutory restrictions on when tactical teams could be deployed, legislators might consider whether excessive deployment of federal tactical teams could be limited through more oversight of how agencies use their teams. Additional oversight might provide federal agencies with an indication of when Congress believes it is acceptable for tactical teams to be deployed without establishing rigid rules for their deployment.

Centralizing Federal Tactical Operations

Some policymakers might consider if it would be more efficient to have one agency be responsible for conducting tactical operations for all federal agencies. This option might make it easier for Congress to conduct oversight of federal tactical operations because all tactical teams would be the responsibility of one federal agency instead of more than a dozen. It might also help promote more effective tactical team operations. It is possible that if one agency were responsible for conducting all tactical operations, the teams would have enough operations to justify officers serving on them full-time. This could potentially mean that officers would receive more training, and the training would be more consistent because it would be overseen by one agency. Also, operations might be conducted in a more consistent manner if they were carried out by one agency.

There are potential drawbacks to a centralized approach, however. There could be questions about whether one agency's tactical teams would be able to conduct the variety of operations for which federal teams are currently used. Would one agency be able to respond in a timely manner to all of the potential calls for service, especially in remote areas? There have been problems in the past with agencies cooperating on criminal investigations, so it is possible that there could be tensions between an agency requesting tactical support and the sending agency providing it.

The centralized approach might also require Congress to provide additional resources to the agency that would be responsible for conducting tactical operations. If the officers serving on the tactical team were full-time, and since the agency would be conducting all tactical operations, it is probable that the agency would have to either replace officers who were assigned to work on the tactical team or hire new officers to serve on the team. However, additional funding for the dedicated agency might not be offset by savings from shuttering other agencies' tactical teams. Data show that most officers serve on tactical teams part-time. As such, if an agency no longer had a tactical team, it would probably not lay off the officer; rather, the officer would probably dedicate his or her time to non-tactical law enforcement responsibilities. Therefore, the agency would probably not reduce its budget by cutting law enforcement officer positions.

Training Requirements

Research on tactical teams at the state and local levels shows the importance of regular training for their members. There are two issues policymakers might consider related to training. First, should all tactical officers who serve on teams be required to participate in a basic tactical team training course provided by the same agency? The Federal Law Enforcement Training Center (FLETC) does not provide a mandatory training course for tactical officers.[47] FLETC does, however, have active shooter, basic tactical medicine, law enforcement rifle, and use of force in service training programs.[48] The concept of all tactical officers receiving basic training from one agency could raise another issue: would this requirement apply to agencies like the FBI, DEA, and Secret Service that currently have their own training academies?

A second issue might be whether there should be any standards for the amount of continuing training tactical officers receive. For example, should there be a minimum number of hours tactical officers should train each month? Should there be requirements for who can provide the training? The literature on tactical teams at the state and local levels raised concerns about tactical teams not training frequently enough and tactical officers receiving training from private organizations or groups of individuals that promote a more militaristic approach to tactical operations (such as receiving training from military special operations personnel).[49]

Potential Issues for Oversight

There are several issues policymakers could consider should Congress hold hearings on how the federal government is using tactical teams. These issues might include the following:

- What types of operations are federal agencies conducting with their tactical teams?
- Where are tactical officers receiving their training? What type of training are they receiving?
- How are decisions made about when to deploy a tactical team?
- What are the results of tactical operations?
- Do agencies have a procedure in place to review operations that were conducted incorrectly (e.g., if a search warrant is served on the wrong residence)? Is there a way for citizens to submit a formal complaint if they feel that they were targeted by an improper tactical operation?

Appendix A. Methodology and Survey Questions

Methodology

CRS developed a brief questionnaire (see below) that was sent to federal agencies with law enforcement personnel. The questionnaire was developed based on a review of the literature on the "militarization" of law enforcement and the proliferation of SWAT teams. Agencies with law enforcement personnel were identified using the most recent Bureau of Justice Statistics (BJS) report on federal law enforcement officers.[50] CRS attempted to contact the 71 agencies identified in the BJS report.[51]

CRS conducted the survey between October 2014 and January 2015. CRS attempted to establish a point of contact (POC) through a congressional or legislative affairs office. When the agency did not have a listed congressional or legislative affairs office, CRS established contact with the agency by calling the number listed on the agency's website. The questionnaire was emailed to the POC on official CRS letterhead. The questionnaire also included a brief introduction that explained the reason for conducting the survey and how the collected data would be used. CRS requested that a response be provided three weeks after the questionnaire was emailed to the POC. CRS followed up with the POC three times at two-week intervals if the agency did not submit a response within the stated deadline. During the week of January 12 CRS sent a final email to POCs at agencies that had not submitted a response asking them to reply to the questionnaire by January 30. Agencies that did not respond by the final deadline were considered to be non-responders.

Response Rate

CRS established contact with 70 agencies that employ law enforcement personnel. The National Archives and Records Administration's Office of the Inspector General (OIG) did not return several voicemail messages left by CRS. CRS received an official response from 68 of the 70 agencies contacted. The U.S. Capitol Police Department and the Internal Revenue Service, Criminal Investigations Division did not respond to the questionnaire. The Department of the Interior's Office of Law Enforcement and Security responded on behalf of the National Parks Service, the Fish and Wildlife Service, and the Bureau of Reclamation (the other agencies with law enforcement personnel within the Department of the Interior responded directly). The response received from the Office of Law Enforcement and Security did not directly address any of the questions in the questionnaire.

Questions

The following questions were sent to the POC for each of the 70 federal agencies CRS asked to respond to the survey:

(1) Does your agency have any designated tactical teams? Members of these teams are recruited, selected, trained, equipped, and assigned to resolve critical incidents involving a threat to public safety which would otherwise exceed the capabilities of traditional law enforcement, first responders, and/or investigative units. These teams might go by a variety of names, including Special Weapons and Tactics (SWAT) teams, tactical response teams, special

response teams, emergency response unit, or active shooter teams. These teams can be comprised of officers or agents who participate on the team on a part-time basis. (If your agency does not have any tactical teams, please provide data on the number of law enforcement officers your agency currently employs, and there is no need to answer any further questions.)

(2) How many tactical teams does your agency have?

(3) How many law enforcement officers does your agency currently employ, and of those, how many serve on tactical teams?

(4) Do law enforcement officers in your agency who serve on a tactical team serve on a full-time or part-time basis? If the tactical teams are staffed with both full-time and part-time members, what proportion of the law enforcement officers who serve on the tactical teams serve part-time?

(5) In which year were the tactical teams identified in question (1) established?

(6) Please provide a brief description of the tactical teams identified in question (1). Such descriptions can include the mission of the teams and the specialized equipment they carry and use.

(7) Does your agency have any regulations or written policies about when or under what circumstances the tactical teams identified in question (1) are deployed?

(8) Under what circumstances does your agency deploy the tactical team(s) identified in question (1) (e.g., barricaded suspect, active shooter, or hostage situations; serving a "high risk" warrant)?

(9) How many times have the tactical teams identified in question (1) been deployed in each of the past 10 fiscal years?

(10) Where do the members of the tactical teams identified in question (1) receive the training required to serve on a tactical team?

(11) On average, in FY2014, how many hours *per month* did law enforcement officers who serve on tactical teams spend on training for tactical operations?

APPENDIX B. SURVEY DATA

The following tables provide data collected by CRS through its survey of federal tactical teams.

Table B-1. Federal Agencies with Tactical Teams, Reported Number of Law Enforcement Officers, and Number of Officers Serving on Tactical Teams

Agency	Responded?	Tactical Teams?	Number of Law Enforcement Officers	Number of Teams	Number of Tactical Officers	Number of Full-Time Tactical Officers
Bureau of Prisons	Yes	Yes	38,251	145	2,592	0
Federal Bureau of Investigation	Yes	Yes	11,750	57	1,250	100
Drug Enforcement Administration	Yes	Yes	5,247	5	48	48
U.S. Marshals Service	Yes	Yes	3,500	1	100	18
Bureau of Alcohol, Tobacco, Firearms, and Explosives	Yes	Yes	2,400	5	258	46
Department of Justice OIG	Yes	No	116	—	—	—
Customs and Border Protection	Yes	Yes	43,300	10	415	395

Table B-1. (Continued)

Agency	Responded?	Tactical Teams?	Number of Law Enforcement Officers	Number of Teams	Number of Tactical Officers	Number of Full-Time Tactical Officers
Immigration and Customs Enforcement	Yes	Yes	12,800	25	480	10
U.S. Secret Service	Yes	Yes	4,600	4	—a	—
Federal Emergency Management Administration	Yes	No	88	—	—	—
Department of Homeland Security OIG	Yes	No	211	—	—	—
National Park Service	No	—	—	—	—	—
Fish and Wildlife Service	No	—	—	—	—	—
Bureau of Indian Affairs	Yes	No	520	—	—	—
Bureau of Land Management	Yes	No	270	—	—	—
Bureau of Reclamation	No	—	—	—	—	—
Department of the Interior OIG	Yes	No	68	—	—	—
Pentagon Force Protection Agency	Yes	Yes	801	1	25	25

Agency	Responded?	Tactical Teams?	Number of Law Enforcement Officers	Number of Teams	Number of Tactical Officers	Number of Full-Time Tactical Officers
Department of Defense OIG	Yes	No	335	—	—	—
Bureau of Diplomatic Security	Yes	Yes	2,024	11	94	94
Department of State OIG	Yes	No	41	—	—	—
National Institute of Standards and Technology	Yes	No	32	—	—	—
National Oceanic and Atmospheric Administration	Yes	No	160	—	—	—
Bureau of Industry and Security	Yes	No	110	—	—	—
Department of Commerce OIG	Yes	No	11	—	—	—
Bureau of Engraving and Printing	Yes	No	114	—	—	—
Internal Revenue Service, Criminal Investigations	No	—	—	—	—	—
U.S. Mint Police	Yes	No	297	—	—	—

Table B-1. (Continued)

Agency	Responded?	Tactical Teams?	Number of Law Enforcement Officers	Number of Teams	Number of Tactical Officers	Number of Full-Time Tactical Officers
Department of the Treasury, Tax Administration	Yes	No	272	—	—	—
Department of the Treasury OIG	Yes	No	24	—	—	—
U.S. Forest Service	Yes	No	640	—	—	—
Department of Agriculture OIG	Yes	No	142	—	—	—
National Institutes of Health	Yes	Yes	98	1	19	0
Food and Drug Administration	Yes	No	233	—	—	—
Health and Human Services OIG	Yes	No	430	—	—	—
Veterans Health Administration	Yes	No	3,590	—	—	—
Department of Veterans Affairs OIG	Yes	No	157	—	—	—

Agency	Responded?	Tactical Teams?	Number of Law Enforcement Officers	Number of Teams	Number of Tactical Officers	Number of Full-Time Tactical Officers
National Nuclear Security Administration	Yes	Yes	1,750	4	170	170
Department of Energy OIG	Yes	No	63	—	—	—
Social Security Administration OIG	Yes	No	287	—	—	—
Department of Housing and Urban Development OIG	Yes	No	199	—	—	—
Department of Labor OIG	Yes	No	166	—	—	—
Department of Transportation OIG	Yes	No	108	—	—	—
Department of Education OIG	Yes	No	78	—	—	—
Amtrak Police	Yes	No	485	—	—	—
U.S. Capitol Police	No	—	—	—	—	—
U.S. Postal Inspection Service	Yes	No	2,100	—	—	—
Administrative Office of the U.S. Courts	Yes	No	4,789	—	—	—

Table B-1. (Continued)

Agency	Responded?	Tactical Teams?	Number of Law Enforcement Officers	Number of Teams	Number of Tactical Officers	Number of Full-Time Tactical Officers
Tennessee Valley Authority	Yes	No	44	—	—	—
Tennessee Valley Authority OIG	Yes	No	21	—	—	—
Federal Reserve Board	Yes	No	143	—	—	—
U.S. Supreme Court	Yes	No	153	—	—	—
National Aeronautic and Space Administration	Yes	Yes	848	2	29	0
National Aeronautic and Space Administration OIG	Yes	No	57	—	—	—
Environmental Protection Agency	Yes	No	183	—	—	—
Environmental Protection Agency OIG	Yes	No	46	—	—	—
Government PublishingOffice	Yes	No	33	—	—	—
Smithsonian National Zoological Park	Yes	No	33	—	—	—

Agency	Responded?	Tactical Teams?	Number of Law Enforcement Officers	Number of Teams	Number of Tactical Officers	Number of Full-Time Tactical Officers
U.S. Postal Service OIG	Yes	No	550	—	—	—
General Services Administration OIG	Yes	No	67	—	—	—
Federal Deposit Insurance Corporation OIG	Yes	No	55	—	—	—
Small Business Administration OIG	Yes	No	34	—	—	—
Office of Personnel Management OIG	Yes	No	34	—	—	—
U.S. Railroad Retirement Board OIG	Yes	No	19	—	—	—
Agency for International Development OIG	Yes	No	31	—	—	—
Nuclear Regulatory Commission OIG	Yes	No	15	—	—	—
Corporation for National and Community Service OIG	Yes	No	5	—	—	—
National Science Foundation OIG	Yes	No	6	—	—	—

Table B-1. (Continued)

Agency	Responded?	Tactical Teams?	Number of Law Enforcement Officers	Number of Teams	Number of Tactical Officers	Number of Full-Time Tactical Officers
National Archives and Records Administration OIG	No	—	—	—	—	—
Government Printing Office OIG	Yes	No	8	—	—	—
Library of Congress OIG	Yes	No	3	—	—	—
Total	**65**	**13**	**145,045**	**271**	**2,888**	**906**

Source: Data collected as a part of CRS's survey of federal tactical teams. Notes: "OIG" stands for "Office of the Inspector General."

a. The U.S. Secret Service reported that the number of agents and officers serving on their tactical teams was "law enforcement sensitive."

Table B-2. Names of Federal Tactical Teams

Agency	Name of Team(s)
Federal Bureau of Investigation (FBI)	Special Weapons and Tactics (56), and Hostage Rescue Team (1)
Bureau of Prisons (BOP)	Special Operations Response Teams (36), and Disturbance Control Teams (109)
Drug Enforcement Administration (DEA)	Foreign Deployed Advisory and Support Teams
U.S. Marshals Service (USMS)	Special Operations Group

Agency	Name of Team(s)
Bureau of Alcohol, Tobacco, Firearms, and Explosives (ATF)	Special Response Teams
Customs and Border Protection (CBP)	Office of Field Operations Special Response Team (1), and Border Patrol Tactical Unit (1 national, 8 regional)
Immigration and Customs Enforcement (ICE)	Homeland Security Investigations Special Response Teams (17), and Enforcement and Removal Operations Special Response Teams (8)
U.S. Secret Service	Counter Assault Team (1), Counter Sniper Branch (1), Emergency Response Team (1), and Hazardous Agent Mitigation Medical Emergency Response (1)
Bureau of Diplomatic Security	Mobile Security Deployments
Pentagon Force Protection Agency	Emergency Response Team
National Institutes of Health (NIH) Police	Special Response Team
National Nuclear Safety Administration (NNSA)	Special Response Teams
National Aeronautic and Space Administration (NASA) Police	Emergency Response Teams

Source: Data collected as a part of CRS's survey of federal tactical teams.

Table B-3. Description of the Role of Federal Tactical Teams

Agency	Description of Tactical Team
Federal Bureau of Investigation (FBI)	Special Weapons and Tactics (SWAT): SWAT teams are specially trained FBI Special Agents who participate in arrests and investigative actions that pose a higher level for potential violence to law enforcement and civilian personnel. Hostage Rescue Team (HRT): HRT is the U.S. government's civilian full-time counterterrorist tactical team. HRT provides enhanced manpower, training, and resources to confront the most complex criminal and terrorism threats faced by the FBI. The team performs a number of national security and law enforcement tactical functions in almost any environment or conditions.
Bureau of Prisons (BOP)	Special Operations Response Teams (SORT): SORT has the responsibility to maintain an effective crisis management program. Crisis management involves the combined effort of several highly trained elements, one of which is the tactical element. While the negotiation process is the primary response, tactical elements are trained and prepared to perform a variety of tactical functions. SORT provides each designated institution with a flexible response to unconventional and high-risk situations. Disturbance Control Teams (DCT): These teams have the responsibility of maintaining effective emergency response procedures and contingency plans for most situations (e.g., fire, work strike, institution disturbance, hostage situation, escape, adverse weather). The specific mission of DCTs is to disperse crowds, move participants, and gain and maintain control of a situation.
Drug Enforcement Administration (DEA)	Foreign Deployed Advisory and Support Teams (FAST): The mission of FAST is to enable DEA to conduct intelligence-driven interdiction operations in support of the U.S. Government's foreign drug policy and enhance U.S. Embassy Country Teams by strengthening the host-nation counterparts' capabilities and expertise through advising, training, and mentorship. FAST personnel perform complex international criminal drug investigations targeting high-level drug trafficking organizations.

Agency	Description of Tactical Team
U.S. Marshals Service (USMS)	Special Operations Group (SOG): SOG is a specially trained and equipped tactical unit deployed in high risk/sensitive law enforcement situations, national emergencies, civil disorders, and natural disasters in support of USMS core missions in all districts and headquarters divisions or as ordered by the U.S. Attorney General.
Bureau of Alcohol, Tobacco, Firearms, and Explosives (ATF)	Special Response Team (SRT): The ATF formed the SRT to manage the risks associated with the investigation and apprehension of violent criminals. The crisis negotiator program has 38 crisis negotiators trained and available to support all SRT operations.
Customs and Border Protection (CBP)	Special Response Team (SRT): SRT was developed to respond to national security incidents, threats to ports of entry, and other significant border security threats. The SRT is trained o resolve critical incidents that are so hazardous and complex, or unusual, that they exceed the capabilities of traditional CBP officers. Border Patrol Tactical Unit (BORTAC): The team provides a trained and highly specialized rapid response unit in order to conduct a wide spectrum of special operations, including counter-drug and other missions with a national security nexus.
Immigration and Customs Enforcement (ICE)	Special Response Teams (SRT): The mission of the ICE SRTs is to conduct high-risk enforcement operations and other specialized duties within the scope of the training and capabilities of its members.
U.S. Secret Service	The Counter Assault Team (CAT): The team provides full-time tactical support for the Presidential Protective Division to protect the President of the United States from significant or organized threats. CAT also provides tactical support to other designated protectees, venues, and National Special Security Events. The Emergency Response Team (ERT): ERT provides the White House and other authorized locations with middle perimeter compound security by initiating a coordinated, tactical response to external penetrations.

Table B-3. (Continued)

Agency	Description of Tactical Team
	The Counter Sniper Team (CS): CS is responsible for providing protection from a long-range single threat and/or a coordinated assault. CS is responsible for providing long-range observation and real-time intelligence information in support of protective details, counter assault teams, and other law enforcement personnel. Counter Sniper Technicians also assist in the identification of aircraft, watercraft, and individuals who are in violation of secure areas. Hazardous Agent Mitigation Medical Emergency Response (HAMMER): The team assists in quickly and safely removing protectees from unsafe, contaminated environments. HAMMER provides appropriate decontamination procedures and emergency medical treatment as required to assist the White House Medical Unit (WHMU), Contingency Medical Officer (CMO), or other higher-level medical providers.
Bureau of Diplomatic Security	Mobile Security Deployments (MSD): MSD provides a secure environment for conducting U.S. foreign policy by providing rapid operational responses to emergency situations. MSD teams operate primarily overseas with limited responsibilities within the United States. Teams are deployed to conduct one of MSD's three primary mission sets: • Security Support Teams (SST) are deployed to posts abroad during periods of immediate threat of terrorist attack, critical levels of violent criminal activity, political crisis, natural disaster, or other unusual events. • Tactical Support Teams (TST), both domestically and abroad, provide support for high-threat protective missions. • Integrated Mobile Training Teams (IMTT) are deployed to provide specialized training at overseas posts. The IMTT provides refresher training for all security elements at posts.

Agency	Description of Tactical Team
Pentagon Force Protection Agency	Emergency Response Team (ERT): The ERT responds when force protection requires unusual displays of public deterrence, when a threat situation requires law enforcement tactical capabilities, or when deadly force may be required. The ERT is trained to isolate high-risk situations and bring them under control quickly, focus on life safety, systematize decisions, and use force only to the extent required to protect the public and the officers involved.
National Institutes of Health (NIH) Police	Special Response Team (SRT): The SRT's mission is to protect the NIH community from internal threats, such as active shooters, and external threats from domestic or foreign terrorists. The SRT is trained in tactics optimized to neutralize threats to Select Agent storage areas, irradiators, patient clinics, and laboratories. The SRT also provides dignitary protection during presidential, congressional, and foreign heads of state visits.
National Nuclear Safety Administration (NNSA)	Special Response Team (SRT): The mission of the SRT is to resolve incidents that require force options that exceed the capability of regular security personnel and/or existing physical security systems. The SRT is trained and equipped to conduct interdiction, interruption, and neutralization operations and containment, denial, recapture, recovery, and pursuit strategies.
National Aeronautic and Space Administration (NASA) Police	Emergency Response Team (ERT): ERT's primary duties consist of a variety of disciplines including, but not limited to, mobile security patrols, investigations, traffic enforcement, and physical security duties/responsibilities. The specialized teams constitute and operate in the event of a high-risk situation.

Source: Data collected as a part of CRS's survey of federal tactical team

Table B-4. Average Number of Training Hours Per Month

Tactical Team	Average Per Month Training Hours
Federal Bureau of Investigation HRT	80
Federal Bureau of Investigation SWAT	32
Drug Enforcement Administration FAST	160
Alcohol, Tobacco, Firearms, and Explosives SRT	13
Pentagon Force Protection Agency ERT	16
Customs and Border Protection SRT	32
U.S. Marshals Service SOG	16
National Aeronautic and Space Administration Police ERT	25
National Nuclear Security Administration SRT	14
National Institutes of Health Police SRT	24
Bureau of Diplomatic Security MSD	55
Immigration and Customs Enforcement SRT	20[a]
Bureau of Prisons SORT	8
Bureau of Prisons DCT	3

Source: Data collected as a part of CRS's survey of federal tactical teams.

Notes: The U.S. Secret Service did not provide an average number of training hours per month. They reported that the number of training hours varies per month based on operational requirements. Customs and Border Protection did not submit data on the average number of training hours for BORTAC.

[a] Immigration and Customs Enforcement reported that their SRTs train between 8 and 32 hours per month. The amount reported in Table B-4 is the median for this range.

Table B-5. Year That Federal Tactical Teams Were Established

Tactical Team	Number of Teams	Year Established
U.S. Secret Service CS	1	1971
U.S. Marshals Service SOG	1	1971
Federal Bureau of Investigation SWAT	56	1973
U.S. Secret Service CAT	1	1979
National Aeronautic and Space Administration Police Kennedy Space Center ERT	1	1979
Bureau of Prisons DCT	109	1982
National Nuclear Security Administration SRT	4	1982
Federal Bureau of Investigation HRT	1	1983
Customs and Border Protection BORTAC	9	1984
U.S. Secret Service ERT	1	1985
Bureau of Prisons SORT	36	1985
Bureau of Diplomatic Security MSD	11	1985
Pentagon Force Protection Agency ERT	1	1989
Bureau of Alcohol, Tobacco, Firearms, and Explosives SRT	5	1996
Immigration and Customs Enforcement SRT	6	1998[a]
National Institutes of Health Police SRT	1	2002
National Aeronautic and Space Administration Police Johnson Space Center ERT	1	2003
U.S. Secret Service HAMMER	1	2004
Drug Enforcement Administration FAST	5	2005
Customs and Border Protection SRT	1	2007
Immigration and Customs Enforcement SRT	11	2005-2013[b]
Immigration and Customs Enforcement ERO	8	2005-2013[c]

Source: Data collected as a part of CRS's survey of federal tactical teams.

[a] ICE reported that its first six ERTs were legacy teams from the U.S. Customs Department (referred to as Warrant Entry Tactical Teams, or WETT) and they were renamed SRT when the program was formalized in 1998.

[b] ICE reported that it established 11 of its 17 SRTs between 2005 and 2013. The agency did not provide a year of establishment for each team.

[c] ICE reported that it established its eight EROs between 2005 and 2013. The agency did not provide a year of establishment for each team.

Table B-6. Reasons for Deploying Tactical Teams

Agency	Reasons Why a Tactical Team Might Deploy
Federal Bureau of Investigation (FBI)	HRT: Supporting high-risk investigations, hostage rescue, barricaded suspects, undercover operations, high-risk arrests, high-risk surveillance, natural disaster response, protection of personnel or dignitaries. SWAT: Serving warrants, supporting high-risk investigations, active shooters, barricaded suspects, protection of personnel or dignitaries.
Bureau of Prisons (BOP)	Hostage rescue, barricaded inmates, institutional disturbances, inmate escapes.
Drug Enforcement Administration (DEA)	Counter-drug operations, assisting foreign drug enforcement agencies with developing their capacity to target drug trafficking organizations.
U.S. Marshals Service (USMS)	Apprehending fugitives, protection of personnel or dignitaries, providing court security, transporting high-risk prisoners, providing witness security, seizing assets, natural disaster response.
Bureau of Alcohol, Tobacco, Firearms, and Explosives (ATF)	Serving warrants, actives hooter, hostage rescue, undercover operations, high-risk surveillance, home barricaded suspects, natural disaster response, protection of personnel or dignitaries.
Customs and Border Protection (CBP)	SRT: Active shooter; high-risk surveillance; protection for personnel or dignitaries; security for special events; motorcade operations; serving warrants; responding to a chemical, biological, radiological, nuclear, and explosive (CBRNE) incident; natural disaster response. BORTAC: High-risk apprehensions, counter-drug operations, security for special events, high-risk surveillance.
Immigration and Customs Enforcement (ICE)	High-risk apprehensions, entering fortified structures.

Agency	Reasons Why a Tactical Team Might Deploy
U.S. Secret Service	The Secret Service did not provide examples of when it steams might be deployed. The agency specified that its teams are always available to respond to a variety of threats in the course of their protective responsibilities.
Bureau of Diplomatic Security	Response to a terrorist incident or an immediate threat of terrorist or criminal activity, natural disaster response.
Pentagon Force Protection Agency	Hostage rescue, high-risk apprehensions, barricaded suspects; protection of personnel or dignitaries, active shooter, security for special events.
National Institutes of Health (NIH) Police	High-risk apprehensions, active shooter, barricaded suspect, hostage rescue, protection of personnel or dignitaries, security during the transportation of select agents and radioactive materials.
National Nuclear Safety Administration (NNSA)	Attacks against any NNSA facilities containing Category I (weapons grade) special nuclear material.
National Aeronautic and Space Administration (NASA) Police	Hostage rescue, terrorist attack, active shooter, barricaded suspect, bus distress alarms.

Source: Data collected as a part of CRS's survey of federal tactical teams.

Table B-7. Number of Reported Deployments of Federal Tactical Teams, FY2005-FY2014

	Fiscal Year									
Agency	**2005**	**2006**	**2007**	**2008**	**2009**	**2010**	**2011**	**2012**	**2013**	**2014**
Bureau of Prisons	—	—	—	—	—	—	—	—	—	—
Federal Bureau of Investigation	840	853	843	954	932	1,004	985	1,009	1,056	1,065
Drug Enforcement Administration	2	5	5	7	9	9	9	10	9	7
U.S. Marshals Service	28	28	28	28	28	28	28	28	28	28
Bureau of Alcohol, Tobacco, Firearms, and Explosives	107	125	196	230	210	250	195	201	193	182
Customs and Border Protection	—	—	2	6	35	167	55	29	83	225
Immigration and Customs Enforcement	—	134	142	150	198	171	253	252	339	398
U.S. SecretService	—	—	—	—	—	—	—	—	—	
Pentagon Force Protection Agency	144	154	165	180	297	240	243	267	201	
Bureau of Diplomatic Security	30	29	33	58	35	36	36	44	53	
National Institutes of Health	—	—	—	—	—	—	—	—	—	
National Nuclear Security Administration	0	0	0	0	0	0	0	0	0	0
National Aeronautic and Space Administration	20	20	20	20	20	20	20	20	20	20
Total	**1,171**	**1,348**	**1,434**	**1,633**	**1,764**	**1,925**	**1,824**	**1,860**	**1,982**	**2,227**

Source: Data collected as a part of CRS's survey of federal tactical teams.

Notes: The Bureau of Prisons and the U.S. Secret Service were not able to provide data on the number of times their tactical teams were deployed each fiscal year. Also, Customs and Border Protection only provided deployment data for their SRTs, not BORTAC. The U.S. Marshals and the National Aeronautic and Space Administration were only able to provide an average annual number of deployments.

End Notes

[1] American Civil Liberties Union, *War Comes Home: The Excessive Militarization of American Policing*, New York, June 2014; Niraj Chokshi, "Militarized Police in Ferguson Unsettles Some; Pentagon Gives Cities Equipment," *Washington Post*, August 14, 2014.

[2] See S. 1441.

[3] See S. 1245 and H.R. 2326.

[4] "Law enforcement personnel" were identified as employees of the agency who are authorized to carry firearms and make arrests.

[5] In this report the terms SWAT, tactical teams, and PPU will be used interchangeably.

[6] National Tactical Officers Association, *SWAT Standards for Law Enforcement Agencies*, September 2008, p. 2.

[7] Ibid.

[8] Peter B. Kraska and Victor E. Kappeler, "Militarizing American Police: The Rise and Normalization of Paramilitary Units," *Social Problems*, vol. 44, no. 1, February 1997, pp. 3-4 (hereinafter, Militarizing American Police).

[9] Peter B. Kraska and Louis J. Cubellis, "Militarizing Mayberry and Beyond: Making Sense of American Paramilitary Policing," *Justice Quarterly*, vol. 14, no. 4, December 1997, p. 627 (hereinafter, Militarizing Mayberry and Beyond).

[10] Abigail R. Hall and Christopher J. Coyne, "The Militarization of U.S. Domestic Policing," *The Independent Review*, vol. 17, no. 4, Spring 2013, p. 489.

[11] Ibid.

[12] Ibid., p. 495.

[13] Ibid., p. 490.

[14] David A. Klinger and Jeff Rojek, *A Multi-method Study of Special Weapons and Tactics Teams: Executive Summary*, final report to the National Institute of Justice, grant award #2000-IJ-CX-0003, August 2008, p. 1 (hereinafter, *A Multi-method Study of Special Weapons and Tactics Teams: Executive Summary*).

[15] Ibid.

[16] Militarizing American Police, p. 6.

[17] Militarizing Mayberry and Beyond, p. 612.

[18] Ibid., p. 613.

[19] Peter B. Kraska, "Militarization and Policing—Its Relevance to 21st Century Police," *Policing*, vol. 1, no. 4, 2007, p. 6 (hereinafter, Militarization and Policing—Its Relevance to 21st Century Police).

[20] American Civil Liberties Union, *War Comes Home: The Excessive Militarization of American Policing*, New York, June 2014, p. 35 (hereinafter, *War Comes Home*).

[21] Ibid.

[22] Ibid., p. 36.

[23] Ibid.

[24] Militarization and Policing—Its Relevance to 21st Century Police, pp 6-7.

[25] Ibid., p. 7.

[26] *A Multi-method Study of Special Weapons and Tactics Teams: Executive Summary*, pp. 12-13.

[27] Ibid., p. 7.

[28] Ibid., p. 14.

[29] *War Comes Home*, p. 32.

[30] Ibid., p. 28.

[31] Ibid., p 27.

[32] *A Multi-method Study of Special Weapons and Tactics Teams: Executive Summary*, p. 5.

[33] Ibid.

[34] Ibid., p. 14.

[35] Militarizing Mayberry and Beyond, p. 609.

[36] Ibid.

[37] Ibid.

[38] Militarizing American Police, p. 13.

[39] Victor E. Kappeler and Peter B. Kraska, "A Textual Critique of Community Policing: Police Adaption to High Modernity," *Policing: An International Journal of Policing Strategies & Management*, vol. 21, no. 2 (1998), p. 306.

[40] The methodology CRS used to survey federal agencies that employ law enforcement personnel to inquire about whether they maintain tactical teams and a list of the questions CRS submitted to these agencies is provided in Appendix A. A list of agencies that responded to the CRS questionnaire can be found in Table B-1.

[41] The National Parks Service (NPS) did not respond to the CRS questionnaire. NPS's website reports that the U.S. Park Police have a SWAT team that was established in 1975; see http://www.nps.gov/subjects/uspp/special-forcesoffice.htm. The U.S. Capitol Police Department also declined to respond to the CRS questionnaire, media reports indicate that the department has a tactical unit called the Containment and Emergency Response Team (CERT); see http://www.usatoday.com/story/news/nation/2013/09/18/navy-yard-capitol-police-swat-team-recalled/2834079/.

[42] The Homeland Security Act of 2002 (P.L. 107-296) transferred the functions, relevant funding, and most of the personnel of 22 agencies and offices to the new Department of Homeland Security (created by the act). It is possible that some of DHS's tactical teams were established as part of a different department.

[43] CBP only provided deployment data for its Special Response Team, which was established in 2007. CBP did not provide deployment data for its Border Patrol Tactical Unit.

[44] The NIH police reported that it did not collect data on the number of times its Special Response Team was deployed prior to 2014.

[45] The most recent BJS report on federal law enforcement officers was released in June 2012 and presents data for 2008. It is available online at http://www.bjs.gov/content/pub/pdf/fleo08.pdf.

[46] See, for example, pp. 27-31 of *War Comes Home*.

[47] Telephone conversation with FLETC on July 22, 2015.

[48] FLETC is the "Nation's primary provider of law enforcement training." FLETC provides training in areas common to all law enforcement officers, such as firearms, driving, tactics, investigations, and legal training. Department of Homeland Security, *Budget-in-Brief, Fiscal Year* 2016, pp. 99-102, http://www.dhs.gov/sites/default/files/publications/FY_2016_DHS_Budget_in_Brief.pdf.

[49] Peter B. Kraska, "Questioning the Militarization of U.S. Police: Critical Versus Advocacy Scholarship," *Policing and Society*, vol. 9, 1999, pp. 141-155.

[50] Brian A. Reaves, *Federal Law Enforcement Officers, 2008*, U.S. Department of Justice, Office of Justice Programs, Bureau of Justice Statistics, NCJ 238250, Washington, DC, June 2012, http://www.bjs.gov/content/pub/pdf/fleo08.pdf.

[51] The BJS report lists 73 agencies with law enforcement personnel. However, the report lists the Library of Congress as having law enforcement personnel. The U.S. Capitol Police Department assumed the duties of the Library of Congress Police Department on October 1, 2009. Also, the report lists two law enforcement agencies for the National Parks Service: The U.S. Park Rangers and the U.S. Park Police. CRS only contacted the National Parks Service to inquire about their tactical teams.

INDEX

D

P

Q

R

S

T